MARCHING TOWARD
MODERATE PROSPERITY

MARCHING TOWARD MODERATE PROSPERITY

THE CHINESE DREAM THROUGH THE EYES OF PUBLIC SERVANTS

HARRY ZIYU HE

NEW DEGREE PRESS

COPYRIGHT © 2021 HARRY ZIYU HE

All rights reserved.

MARCHING TOWARD MODERATE PROSPERITY

The Chinese Dream Through the Eyes of Public Servants

ISBN   978-1-63676-933-2 *Paperback*

            978-1-63676-997-4 *Kindle Ebook*

            978-1-63730-101-2 *Ebook*

To those chasing the Chinese Dream

CONTENTS

———

Hefei at night. Photo by the author

ACKNOWLEDGMENTS

This book has its origin in an independent research project
I conducted in the summer of 2019. As a college sophomore
eager to apply the lessons I had learned in class, I plunged
into weeks of intensive fieldwork with interviews and participant observations. I finished my research paper in early
September, boarded a plane to London, and began my study
abroad journey at Oxford. I put aside the project, hoping to
return to it when the timing was right. When I was presented
with an opportunity to write a book while quarantining at
my apartment near Georgetown, I knew it was the right time
to resume this research project.

As a first-time author, I could not have completed this book
without the help of many. First, I want to thank my mentors at Georgetown University. Words cannot express my
gratitude for the support I have received from Dr. Den-
nis McNamara on this project from the beginning. I first
approached Dr. McNamara with a proposal to conduct an
independent research in China over the summer after com-
pleting his class on East Asian economy and society. After
asking me my research interests, he pointed my way toward

the *danwei* system, which then became the central topic of my research paper and a key component of this book. I am also indebted to my teachers and research mentors at Georgetown, including Dr. Kristen Looney, Dr. Christine Kim, Dr. Evan Medeiros, Dr. Oriana Mastro, Dr. Lynn Kuok, Dr. Jordan Sand, Dr. Diana Kim, Dr. Kevin Doak, and Dr. Yoshiko Mori, for kindling my interest in Asian studies and teaching me everything from Chinese foreign policy to Japanese history. They also provided me with constant support and valuable guidance during my undergraduate career.

I would additionally like to thank Dr. Amanda Palmer, Nicholas Martindale, and Andrew Elliott for teaching me the theoretical knowledge and quantitative research tools that strongly benefited my research. I also wish to express my gratitude toward my tutorial mentors, including Dr. Giulio Pugliese, Dr. Hugh Whittaker, and Peng Sheng, who have challenged me to excel both as a student and as a budding researcher.

I am incredibly grateful for the support I have received from the Georgetown Prep community. I would like to thank numerous faculty members, including John Glennon, Erik Maginnis, Dr. Stephen Ochs, Benjamin Williams, Kevin Buckley, Dacque Tirado, Thomas Gigot, Billy Falatko, John Krambuhl, and Robert Barry, who not only guided me throughout my four years of high school but also showed incredible support for my book journey. I have also received generous encouragement from my friends from Prep, including Brian Dolan, Jimmy Roche, William McAvoy, Henry Furlong, Max Metcalfe, Tinghui She, Brian Long, Kevin McGarry, and Ned Flanagan.

To those who voluntarily participated in my research, I also owe a debt of gratitude. They have trusted me with their stories and helped make this book possible.

I am indebted to the support I have received from my coaches and editors at New Degree Press, especially Prof. Eric Koester, Jordan Waterwash, and P. Richelle White. My gratitude also goes to Gjorgji Pejkovski and Stefan Mancevski who helped me turn my idea into the stellar book cover.

Friends and family have also shared their love, support, and confidence that I would finish this daunting project. I would like to personally thank Yifan Lyu, Stanley Huang, Ariel Huang, Litai (Tony) Wei, Zhihang Wang, Yuchang Li, Shuxiao Miao, Jennifer Wen, Jianguo Jiang, John Almaguer, Vincent Tran, Letitia Wu, Emily Xue, Yueyang Huang, Xiuping Guo, Dengsheng Liu, Guoze Shen, Xinhe Shen, Wei Shen, Xuelian Liu, Juncai (Tina) Luo, Baocheng Zhang, Xinyu Hong, Xueling Hua, Lei He, Qiong Zhang, Huizi Mao, Min Zhang, Suping Wang, Yichen Wang, Xiaofeng Xu, Zhanchi Wang, Zihe Wang, Jinwei Chen, Feng Chen, Junling Chen, Fengling Chen, Bin Miao, Zhenyi (Leslie) Li, Miaoyun (Miao) Li, Caixia Ni, Gang Li, Fuan He, Chunhua Chen, An He, Daiyan Wan, Zhishang Zhou, Lihang Zhou, Lifan Zhou, Yaping Fan, Bin Xie, Yan Wang, Yutao Xie, Yuxia Xie, Yuheng Xie, Yiqiu Shen, Lingping Wu, Xijuan Zhu, Liangjun Cheng, Tingyuan (Lucas) Cheng, Qi Zhang, and Zhuo Chen. Miles Oliver and Mitchell Oliver have long been my brothers since I first arrived in the US and have been there for me every step along the way. Zhaorui (Eric) Ding, Cheryl (Qingqin) Yang, Ziyang Wei, and Yuanyi Zhang showed tremendous support by sharing my book and stories with friends and colleagues. I also owe a special debt to Floris (Xujia) Liu, Shawn (Weichen) Lu, Rohan Dalvi, and Jackson Barkstrom for organizing and participating in my book talks.

My incredible and loving parents, Jun He and Danmei Chen, have supported all my decisions and provided me with incredible assistance during my onsite and remote fieldwork research. They, along with my grandparents, Maolin Chen, Xiuying Zhang, and Lehua He, and my cousins, Chenfei (Olivia) Xia, Yunke (Lucy) Sun, Mujie Zhang, and Zichen (Blanche He), have also been the biggest cheerleaders throughout my life.

My girlfriend and best friend, Huaan (Amber) Liao, has been with me in this journey since the beginning. She was the one who first told me about the opportunity to write a book—without her my dream would not have become a reality. I will forever be grateful to her for being with me through the highs and lows and for reminding me what is important at the end of a bad day.

INTRODUCTION
A NEW TALE OF CHINA

"Don't forget to upload the documents. I sent them over email. Get it done by five today."

Mr. Chen's supervisor, Mrs. Zhu, interrupted us and peeked her head through the door while we were chatting. Mr. Chen forced a smile on his face and responded full of energy and enthusiasm.

"Got it! Right away!"

The second Mrs. Zhu walked away, Mr. Chen turned toward me and sighed. "This is the life of civil servants in China. Life here is so monotonous and boring. I honestly don't know how you can write a book on this."

Before I could justify myself, Mr. Chen had positioned himself in front of his computer and resumed both working and complaining.

"My daily life feels like dancing with my feet shackled," he said.

I never expected a witty, energetic soul only a few years my senior could exude such a strong sense of pessimism toward the future. A first-generation college graduate, Mr. Chen had hoped education could change his destiny, and from the conventional standard in China, he has succeeded at his current stage in life, given his background. On the verge of turning thirty, he has a stable, reputable career and an apartment in his name. Deep down, however, Mr. Chen remains unsatisfied.

"No matter how far I look into the future, I see almost no uncertainty. It feels like my life has been completely determined the moment I accepted this job."

Worn down by the mundane, trivial, and unrewarding tasks of civil service, Mr. Chen felt trapped by an invisible cage that sucked away his joy, energy, and enthusiasm day by day. Though he longed for freedom and adventure, Mr. Chen was dragged down by a sense of stability and security, as well as the mortgage that would render him a "slave of his own apartment" for the next decade.

Given China's booming economy and the widespread expectation among Chinese citizens for a better future, Mr. Chen's sentiment may seem bizarre, but his experience is not unique. In fact, there is a concrete yet often overlooked dissonance between the belief that China's economic boom means greater prosperity for all and the pessimism shared by millions of Chinese youths, including Mr. Chen. His story—their story—is not one of failure but of misfortune.

The story of China's unprecedented economic growth in the past four decades is nothing short of a miracle. It is difficult to imagine that Westerners once thought of China as a poor, backward country led by a ruthless, cantankerous leader—much as we picture North Korea today. In every respect, China is living the dream of economic boom and prosperity. In less than forty years, China has transformed from an impoverished country devastated by a planned economy to the second largest GDP in the world with world-class infrastructure and bedazzling skylines. The rapid economic growth has also profoundly impacted daily lives of Chinese citizens. Between 1990 and 2019, real GDP per capita rose from $318 to $10,262.[1] In 2018, Chinese consumers at home and abroad spent 770 billion RMB ($115 billion) on luxury items—one-third of global spending.[2]

THE BIRTH OF THE CHINESE DREAM

In 2013, Chinese President Xi Jinping used the phrase "Chinese Dream (中国梦)" to describe a set of personal and national ethos for the ultimate goal of revitalizing the great Chinese nation. Although the official explanation emphasizes the ideas of collective effort, socialism, and national glory, and downplays the pursuit of individual dreams, for

---

1   "GDP per Capita (Current US$) – China," The World Bank Data, accessed August 5, 2020.
2   Lan Luan et al, *China Luxury Report 2019: How Young Chinese Consumers are Reshaping Global Luxury* (Shanghai: McKinsey Greater China's Apparel, Fashion and Luxury Group, 2019), 4.

most Chinese citizens, especially the burgeoning middle class, grandiose dreams such as "national rejuvenation (中华民族伟大复兴)" seem much more nebulous than the tangible goal of personal success.

Against the backdrop of a booming economy, social mobility through hard work has become a tangible possibility, and at the individual level, the Chinese Dream has a clear connection to the American Dream, which espouses a similar idea of advancement through individual efforts. In the reform era, Deng Xiaoping's slogan "To Get Rich is Glorious" replaced the socialist mentality emphasizing collectivism. Suddenly, finding ways to earn money and bragging about one's fortune were no longer viewed as counterrevolutionary and treasonous. Encouraged by this new calling, many Chinese ventured overseas to seek their American Dream as first-generation immigrants in a distant land across the Pacific. Many more grasped onto new economic opportunities within China and realized their Chinese Dream. In less than a generation's time, China transformed from an insular, mysterious territory to a prosperous land where money flows and dreams come true.

While the concept of the Chinese Dream may resemble a tangible reality to the fortunate few, for many others, it remains—at best—a myth and—at worst—pure propaganda. Much like the American Dream carries different meaning for people with different racial, gender, and socioeconomic backgrounds, the Chinese Dream is not one of equal opportunity. Since the early days of the Reform and Opening Campaign, Chinese leaders have envisioned that economic reform would ultimately bring prosperity for all by allowing "some people to get rich first (让一部分人先富起来)"—a model similar to Reagan's trickle-down economics but with the socialist air of egalitarianism. In the past forty years, China has indeed allowed some people to get rich first; in 2019, China had over three hundred billionaires, ranked second after the US, but the promise of prosperity for all is nowhere near this amount.[3]

AN UNEQUAL SUCCESS

Though the economic reform has surely benefited even the most impoverished households in China, acute economic and social inequalities paint a gloomy portrayal of the Chinese Dream.

In May 2020, Premier Li Keqiang revealed the disheartening fact that over 600 million Chinese—almost half of the entire population—survive on less than 1,000 RMB per month ($150).[4] In comparison, Beijing Ministry of Human Resources and Social Security reports that municipal average monthly salaries exceed 7,800 RMB ($1,170) in 2018, with income levels in downtown districts climbing as high as 15,655 RMB ($2,348) according to the municipal Bureau of Statistics.[5] As China underwent rapid urbanization, modernization, and industrialization, the gap between urban and

---

3   This number excludes Hong Kong, Macau, and Taiwan. See Jonathan Ponciano, "The Countries with the Most Billionaires," Forbes, April 8, 2020.

4   "国务院总理李克强回答中外记者提问 (Premier Li Keqiang Answers Questions from Chinese and Foreign Journalists)," Xinhua News, May 28, 2020.

5   "北京城镇单位年人均工资94258元 (Annual Average Salary in Beijing Reaches 94,258 RMB)," Xinhua News, May 31, 2019; 北京市统计局

rural areas widened, and this urban-rural duality is receiving increasing attention from domestic and foreign observers and policy makers. In 2009, a World Bank report revealed that 99 percent of China's poor come from rural areas.[6]

The urban-rural divide, however, did not fully capture the intensity of China's social and economic stratification. China's economic development does not simply favor the cities over the rural countryside; it prioritizes a handful of coastal metropolises over the vast inland regions not as favorable to conducting international trade and commerce. Thus, a sharp contrast emerges between what I term "metropolitan China"—first-tiered cities such as Beijing, Shanghai, and Shenzhen, and "urban China"—and second- and third-tiered cities such as Hefei, where Mr. Chen lives.

As most of the success stories about China's unprecedented economic miracle are concentrated in metropolitan China, urban China and its residents are frequently overlooked in academic research and news reports. At the same time, however, citizens of urban China have a lot to say about China's economy and society. Like Mr. Chen, most of them are well educated, economically independent, and well connected. In other words, they are the quintessential Chinese middle-class—so if they are not living the Chinese Dream, what does this say about the Chinese society?

(Beijing Bureau of Statistics), 北京区域统计年鉴 2019 (*Beijing Statistical Yearbook 2019*) (Beijing: Beijing Bureau of Statistics, 2019).

6   Poverty Reduction and Economic Management Department, *From Poor Areas to Poor People: China's Evolving Poverty Reduction Agenda: An Assessment of Poverty and Inequality in China* (Beijing: The World Bank, 2009), 49.

A native of Hefei, I did not grow up with the conscious belief my city was in any way inferior to megacities such as Shanghai and Beijing. Surely Shanghai is more cosmopolitan, modern, and spectacular, but Hefei has its unique charms. I only realized I was living in a different world from my peers in Beijing and Shanghai when I came to the US for high school. Though we are all international students from China, my hometown had a lot to say about how other Chinese students perceived my socioeconomic background and even how well (or not) I should speak English. My heritage did not become a source of pride. When the admission office placed me out of the traditionally-mandatory English as a second language (ESL) program, some of my Chinese peers voiced strong protest. Arguing we received similar marks on the Test of English as a Foreign Language (TOEFL) exam and believing some nobody from Hefei could not have spoken better English, they speculated whether my family had bribed school officials for preferential treatments.

The direct prejudice and intentional bias I faced early in my time in the US contributed far less to my sense of inferiority than did the social and institutional circumstances into which I had naively landed. Most of the other Chinese students had come to US high schools from middle- to upper-class families in China's coastal metropolises. Before arriving in the US, they had already formed dense and intricate social networks that weren't accessible to an outsider like me. Many had attended middle school together or shared a counselor or tutor. I was fifteen years old, in a strange country, and had little in common with my Chinese peers. Fitting into their cliques often meant sacrificing a part of me that defines my origin.

This gap between "urban China" which Hefei represents and "metropolitan China" became clearer to me when I returned home the summer after my junior year of high school. During reunions with my former classmates, almost all of them expressed a strong desire to go to either Beijing, Shanghai, Hangzhou, or Guangzhou for college. Coastal metropolises such as Shanghai are highly glorified and romanticized.

Their conviction tells a convincing yet disturbing story. It seems the Chinese Dream only belongs to those who find their ways and establish their roots in the metropolises, but not all those that went had the same opportunity. While graduates from prestigious universities often enjoy similar opportunities as local talents, those without such educational background face a myriad of obstacles. The strict household registration (户口) system, for example, essentially limits free migration within China. High living costs also deter many young people from middle-class backgrounds to find a living within these metropolises. So what about people like Mr. Chen? What does the Chinese Dream mean for those who end up in second-tiered cities such as Hefei, or worse?

In this book, I wish to answer this question about the Chinese Dream by conducting a case study on public servants in Hefei. I refine my research subjects to civil servants to construct a reliable and well-defined sample that best conforms to the traditional image of the middle class. More importantly, within China's unique context as a market economy governed by socialism of Chinese characteristics, public employees like Mr. Chen stand at the intersection between traditional values, historical experience of socialism, and the relatively new phenomenon of marketization and privatization. By studying this unique group of people in a part of China rarely explored, I hope to portray a different image of contemporary Chinese society along with my personal stories, experience, and insights.

We live in a world where China's miraculous economic performance contrasts with slow economic recovery of Western democracies. Against this backdrop, a more comprehensive understanding of China is important and even imperative. The gap differentiation between "metropolitan China" and "urban China" can no longer be overlooked. China has sought to address the widely different paces of development between the coastal and inland regions. Since the mid-2010s, second- and third-tiered cities have grown at tremendous, unprecedented paces to emulate, if not, catch up to, first-tiered metropolises. At the same time, "urban China" is also home to the majority of China's middle-class households. These middle-class citizens not only drive China's economic growth but also determine the future trajectory of the country. Studying "urban China" thus offers us a unique lens into the reality of China that is relevant to the Chinese people, who care more about their mortgage payments and children's education than the annual GDP growth rate or how many Chinese entrepreneurs are on the Forbes lists.

The story I tell in this book is not a new or exceptional one. It is happening to millions of people in China every day and has been happening to them for decades; however, it will likely be a novel tale for you. For readers interested in learning more about China from a perspective that examines the individual rather than the polity of the economy as a whole, this book will hopefully present you with a new way to look at China.

This book does not look at the top elites who have long dominated books and newspaper articles praising China's economic growth, nor the most destitute members of Chinese society that have received growing domestic and international attention. I will look at those in the middle and present to you a new image of China through the stories of a group of people whose experiences may seem foreign, but their hopes, fears, and dreams are not so different, or unfamiliar, to you and I.

PART ONE

SETTING THE STAGE

中国人民站起来了。

毛泽东 1949年9月21日于全国政协会议第一届全体会议

The Chinese people have stood up.

CHAPTER 1

ON THE CHINESE DREAM

———

On a summer afternoon in 2013, my mother took me to a new spotlight in town that had captured local media attention. As a fourteen-year-old boy who only wanted to spend my summer relaxing at home or going on adventures with friends, I was reluctant to go on this unplanned shopping trip. I couldn't understand the fuss other visitors made over luxury brand shops like Burberry and Gucci. But then I laid my eyes on a luxury brand store that captured my attention. And I discovered it in the food court. Welcome to Hefei, Häagen-Dazs. Seventeen years after the brand first branched out to China, Hefei finally had a Häagen-Dazs store.

When a popsicle cost as little as 0.5 RMB ($0.08) and a high-end Unilever Cornetto 5 RMB ($0.80), Häagen-Dazs's 30 RMB ($4.64)-a-scoop ice cream is nothing short of luxury. The exotic name, fancy packaging, and famous ad slogan, "If you love her, treat her to Häagen-Dazs," all stood as testaments to its status as the glorified symbol of the Western world. Before the first Häagen-Dazs stored opened in Yintai Center, I could only find prepackaged cups of this deluxe ice cream—which only comes in Vanilla, Strawberry, and

Chocolate—stacked in a separate, locked frozen shelf in foreign supermarkets such as the German chain Metro; so when I ordered myself a scoop of blueberry ice cream, I was tasting the modern, mysterious world lying beyond the ocean I would soon become part of.

The spotlight that became my favorite place in Hefei was a recently built shopping mall located at the center of the downtown area. A new attraction in town, the Yintai Center stood out as a symbol of cosmopolitan modernity in juxtaposition with the first municipal department store that has stood around the corner for seven decades.

Häagen-Dazs is no longer a rare sight at Hefei. As foreign luxuries, from Japan's *kaiseki* meals and high-end steakhouses to designer brands such as Tiffany & Co. and Cartier are no longer strangers to Hefei citizens, Häagen-Dazs has long ceased to serve as the symbol of Western culture.

INFRASTRUCTURE AND ECONOMY

The radical transformation in Hefei's social and economic landscape came as a result of the shift to what I term the "HOPSCA economy (综合体经济)." HOPSCA—a novel term denoting hotel, office, park, shopping mall, club, and apartment servicing commercial, business, residential, and entertainment purposes—has become the new and dominant trend of urban development in China. Though urban complexes that fully incorporate all six sections of HOPSCA are rarely seen outside first-tiered cities such as Beijing, Shanghai, and Guangzhou, less extensive forms, mostly excluding parks, and clubs, are frequently found in second-tiered cities such as Hefei.

In the late 2000s, urban complexes began to mushroom throughout Hefei, first in historic downtown and later in every corner of the city. In 2016, Hefei opened the Wanda Cultural Tourism City, the largest HOPSCA the city has ever built, occupying forty hectares, the equivalent of seventy-five football fields. The new HOPSCA features a theme park, an indoor water park, a hotel district, a shopping mall, and extensive residential quarters.

Hefei's transformation proved successful. In 2000, Hefei was not even regarded as a proper city with its ¥32.5 billion GDP ranked beyond eighty nationally. By 2009, Hefei's rank climbed to forty-nine, and in the latest data, Hefei is ranked as the twenty-first largest GDP in China and joined the ranks of fourteen other "new first-tiered cities," an indicator designed by the *Caijing* magazine.

Hefei's success story was not an exception in China. The country's economic miracle in the past four decades witnessed the transformation of hundreds of towns and cities, starting with the costal metropolises and gradually spreading to more inland cities throughout China.

Multibillion companies such as Wanda and Yintai that constructed several urban complexes in Hefei have accomplished the same in a dozen other cities. Hefei is no more than a follower among many that sought to emulate the success of Beijing and Shanghai, albeit a more successful one than many of its peers due to favorable central policies and bold local initiatives. In fact, Hefei's achievements reflect and represent China's success story on the global stage as a backward economy that quickly rose to modernity and prosperity.

The economic success of the nation and its individual cities represent the pursuit of the Chinese Dream. Although a relatively new term promoted by the current Chinese President Xi Jinping since 2013, the Chinese Dream is a reinterpretation and rebranding of a century-long goal of "national rejuvenation (民族复兴)" deeply embedded in the Chinese consciousness for more than a century. This call for revitalizing the Chinese nation seeks to shed the shadow of the century of humiliation (百年国耻) that China suffered at the hands of so-called "barbaric" imperialists between 1840 and 1945 and restore China to the rightful place economically, politically, and militarily.

The collective orientation of the Chinese Dream narrative stemming from the national struggle for prosperity does not conflict with the individual pursuit of personal success and advancement. Until the late 1970s, domestic conditions—be it wars or collectivist ideology—had precluded such personal endeavors save the most powerful or wealthy. The Opening and Reform campaign launched in 1978 introduced Chinese citizens to new opportunities.

With economic privatization, a new Chinese middle class emerged. For the first time in decades, if not centuries, China's domestic environment presented a tangible path of social mobility and economic prosperity. The effects of China's sweeping economic reform not only benefited the elites in power and adventurist spirits but also average citizens in

China who witnessed the unprecedented transformation of their surroundings and their rapidly growing purchasing power on a global level.

The inroads made by renowned luxury brands in China's second-tiered cities such as Hefei have demonstrated the purchasing power of China's middle-class citizens. Few multinational companies—from technology giants such as Apple to luxury retailers such as Christian Dior—can afford to turn away or ignore this formidable group, especially the younger generation within it. In 2012, China overtook Japan as the largest luxury market, compelling Western designers to release unique products inspired by Chinese motifs catering to the expanding market. By 2019, China accounted for 33 percent of the global luxury market and is projected to increase its share to 46 percent by 2025.[7]

EDUCATION

The personal Chinese Dream also features expanding educational opportunities for China's middle-class citizens. Once a treasured scarcity, university education is no longer a distant dream for many Chinese students. In 1990, China's tertiary education gross enrollment rate barely exceeded 3.8 percent, approximately a quarter of the global average. By 2019, college enrollment rate had climbed to 51.6 percent, outstripping the global average of 38 percent.[8] China still lags far

---

7 Claudia D'Arpizio et al, *Luxury Goods Worldwide Market Study, Fall-Winter 2018* (Boston: Bain & Company, 2019), 1, 3, 24.

8 "2019年全国教育事业发展统计公报 (2019 Report on the Development of National Education Work)," Ministry of Education of the People's Republic of China, published May 20, 2020.

behind many developed countries largely due to unequal access to education between urban and rural populations. Rural students still suffer from significant disadvantages in the education system, but for most young people with urban backgrounds, attending universities is no longer an impossible feat.

At the same time, overseas education is becoming more popular among students from second- and even third-tiered cities. Though students from first-tiered cities still form the main driving force behind China's massive study abroad cohort, their counterparts from cities such as Hefei have also joined their ranks.

Growing competition for overseas educational opportunities has compelled many Chinese parents to send their children abroad at much younger ages. Today, Chinese students are no longer a rare sight in American high schools.

In 2013, I flew to the US with 23,794 other Chinese high schoolers, ready to embark on a new journey in a foreign land. I was delighted and slightly surprised to find many of my peers also hailed from middle-class backgrounds like myself. For many of us who received no funding or sponsorship from our schools in the US or the Chinese government back home, our parents' ability to afford our tuition and living costs attests to the prosperity achieved by China's middle class.

The story of China's economic miracles and tales of the growing wealth and influence of China's middle-class citizens foster an expectation, both within and outside China, that everyone, especially the well-educated youth, must be living his or her personal Chinese dream. For many, the assumption rings true. Despite its recent economic slowdown, China is still the land full of opportunity. Among overseas Chinese students, going back home is becoming an increasingly appealing option especially as Western countries, especially the US, tighten immigration rules.

THOSE LEFT BEHIND
Is the Chinese Dream a reality for all?

The simple answer is no. The sharp economic and social disparity between urban and rural China means that success belongs only to urban Chinese citizens and the fortunate few with rural backgrounds.

In terms of education, urban Chinese students are eight times more likely to receive a university education then their rural counterparts, twelve times more likely to attend a top-one hundred university, and forty-three times more likely to enroll in Tsinghua or Beijing University.[9] Given the unequal path of economic development, China's sharp rural-urban divide is not a new discovery. In fact, the assumption on the individual Chinese Dream predicates on the premise that excludes the rural population that has been largely left behind and reflects exclusively China's urban middle class.

---

9   Hongbing Li et al, "Unequal Access to College in China: How Far Have Poor, Rural Students Been Left Behind?" *The China Quarterly,* no. 211 (March 2015): 195.

Discrimination based on ethnicity presents another obstacle for ethnic minorities on their path to success. Though the Chinese government still reject these allegations as ungrounded lies, the international community is no stranger to the oppression of ethnic minorities in China exhibiting desire for greater autonomy, especially the Uighurs in the northwest and the Tibetans in the southwest. Even the more modest "model minority," such as the Mongols and the Hui people, are not treated on par with the Han majority.

Put aside for a moment discrimination based on ethnicity and focus on the very core of China's middle class—urban, well-educated citizens belonging to the Han majority. Through that lens, is the Chinese Dream a tangible reality or merely a constructed myth? Do the tales of social mobility and personal success belong to the majority of the population or are they a privilege reserved for the elite? Does the Chinese Dream have the same meaning for men and women or does it favor one and exclude the other?

My goal with this book is to present you a facet of China's complex society. By doing so, I hope to help you grasp a better understanding of the country that still remains unfamiliar to many, both within and outside China. As the world heads into a direction of increasing competition and confrontation between China and Western countries, an accurate, or at least nonprejudicial, view on China and its people is essential to avoid unnecessary conflicts and make judicious judgments.

The question I raise may seem rather trivial in the face of China's grand strategy and US-China relations, but how Chinese society functions and how Chinese citizens think and perceive their surrounding environments is fundamental to understanding China's goals, interests, and behaviors. In other words, the personal Chinese Dream is fundamentally tied to Xi's national Chinese Dream, which dictates China's aspirations and the actions Beijing is willing to take to fulfill them.

CHAPTER 2

PUBLIC SERVANTS IN CHINA

———

Growing up, I never understood my mother's career. Though she always instructed me to put down "engineer" as her occupation in any school registration form that required parental information, her flexible schedule and the mysterious work she did from behind her desk puzzled me.

It certainly did not help when my mother told me she worked as a "public servant," or "公务员" (which literally translates to "staff [managing] public affairs"). I did, however, sense public service was a reputable and prestigious path—my aunt wanted my cousin to become one and a family friend urged his son to marry one. Still, it would take years for me to fully comprehend the meaning and significance of public service.

Public servants are no strangers to Western societies, but it is nevertheless beneficial and essential to lay down some definitions and familiarize ourselves with the design of this study. As suggested by its literal definition, a "public servant" in China is a "staff member in charge of designated public affairs responsibilities who belongs to the state's administrative system and receives salaries and benefits from state finance."[10]

As a political institution, the public service system in China reflects the country's political environment as a one-party authoritarian state. For example, the Chinese political system does not differentiate politicians from career bureaucrats, meaning all government posts—from the president at the top to a county clerk at the bottom—belong to the same twenty-seven-rank, hierarchical system. China also holds no real election for any of its government posts, so all positions within the system are intimately connected. All senior political figures in Beijing commence their careers as low-ranking bureaucrats in national ministries or local politicians from various provinces. Ambitious politicians must rise through the ranks of civil service.

Chinese political structure, though important, has little bearing on the lives of entry-level civil servants. Instead, what we should focus on is the socialist work unit, or *danwei* (单位), system. One cannot understand public servants in China without first investigating the *danwei* system.

DANWEI: A DEFINITION

One of the most ubiquitous yet mysterious terms in the Chinese lexicon, *danwei* defines an essential aspect of daily life

---

10 "中华人民共和国公务员法 (Civil Servant Law of the People's Republic of China)," *Xinhua News*, December 30, 2018.

in urban China. At a societal level, the *danwei* system made the miraculous economic transformation possible in the past four decades. At an individual level, *danwei* guarantees its employees various benefits, subsidiaries, and social capitals denied to those outside the system.[11] *Danwei* also wields significant political control through reward and punishment mechanisms and unilateral persuasion through the Communist party, contributing to the highly organized social order in contemporary China.

The first obstacle in analyzing the *danwei* system is its definition. It is a word many use but few can accurately define. When getting to know someone we have just met, Chinese frequently ask, "What *danwei* are you from (你哪个单位来的)?" When we talk about our place of business, some Chinese prefer precise terms such as company (公司) or school (学校); more commonly, we opt for the more generic term *danwei*. And when parents express their wish for their children to have a secured, stable career, they say they want them to work in "a good *danwei* (好单位)." In each of these examples, *danwei* refers to a vocation. The difference in connotation is nuanced. In the second example, *danwei* refers to a place of business, but in the first and third examples, it is an identity or a career path.

---

11   Xiaobo Lü and Elizabeth J. Perry, "Introduction," in *Danwei: The Changing Chinese Workplace in Historical and Comparative Perspective,* ed. Xiaobo Lü and Elizabeth J. Perry (New York: M. E. Sharpe, 1997), 3; He Zhongda and Lü Bin, "中国单位制度社会功能的变迁 (Evolution of the *Danwei* System's Societal Functions)," 城市问题 (*Urban Problems*) 26, no 11 (November 2007): 48.

Even within the more precise definition denoting a place of business, *danwei* carries two definitions. The broader one refers to all organized workplaces.[12] The narrower definition, which I use in this book, only refers to the publicly owned work units—government agencies, public institutes such public schools and hospitals, and state-owned enterprises (SOEs).[13]

THE DANWEI SYSTEM: A SOCIALIST INSTITUTION

The amorphous definition and connotation of *danwei* emerged out of a series of ongoing institutional reforms in China over the past four decades. Before the Reform and Opening (改革开放) campaign that redefined China's social and economic landscapes, the entire urban population, with few exceptions, was organized, governed, and managed by the state through individual work units. The state maintained absolute control over the economy and the society. Consequently, all urban entities—whether factories or government departments—were organized into individual work units. Within the "state-*danwei*-individual" framework that characterized the structure of management and mobilization in urban China during the Socialist era, scholars have concluded a condition of organized dependence between

---

12 This definition is used officially in yearbooks published by the Bureau of Statistics at the national, provincial, and municipal levels.

13 Li Hanlin, 中国单位社会: 议论、思考与研究 (*Thoughts on Chinese Work-unit Society*) (Shanghai: Shanghai People's Publishing House, 2004), 1. Bray and Lü and Perry used similar definitions in their own work. See David Bray, *Social Space and Governance in Urban China: the Danwei System from Origin to Reform* (Stanford: Stanford University Press, 2005), 3-4; Lü and Perry, "Introduction," 5. This definition is used as equivalent to the *danwei* system, as oppose to private enterprises called "*gongsi*."

employees and their respective work units.[14] Work units not only serve a "political-statist function" of mobilization and monitoring but also a "social-communal function" of economic and social welfare.[15] At the height of *danwei*'s power during the Socialist era, this unique logic of organization made it a special case of what Erving Goffman labels as "total institution."[16]

A *danwei* office in Hefei. Photo by the author.

---

14 Li Hanlin and Li Lulu, 中国的单位组织: 资源、权力与交换 (*China's Danwei System: Resource, Power, and Exchange*) (Beijing: Life Bookstore Publishing, 2019), 4-7; Li Lulu, "论 '单位' 研究 (Danwei Study)," *Sociological Studies* 17 no. 5 (May 2002): 23-32.

15 Rudra Sil, "The Russian 'Village in the City' and Stalinist System of Enterprise Management: The Origins of Worker Alienation in Soviet State Socialism," in *Danwei: The Changing Chinese Workplace in Historical and Comparative Perspective*, ed. Xiaobo Lü and Elizabeth J. Perry (New York: M. E. Sharpe, 1997), 115. This is especially true prior to the Opening and Reform campaign in 1978 and the 1990s *danwei* reform.

16 Erving Goffman, *Asylum: Essays on the Social Situations of Mental Patients and Other Inmates* (New Brunswick: Aldine Transaction, 2009), xxi-xxii.

Traditionally used to characterize prison and asylum, a total institution is "a place of residence and work where a large number of like-situated individuals...together lead an enclosed, formally administered round of life."[17] While focusing on two special types of total institution characterized by "involuntary membership"—prison and mental hospitals—Goffman identifies a type of total institution "established...to pursue some worklike task."[18] The central feature of a total institution, thus, is to "breakdown [the] barriers ordinarily separating...three spheres of life...sleep, play, and work."[19]

In pre-reform China, iron gates and cement walls of each work unit marked the boundaries of each mini society.[20] Within each, *danwei* offered secured lifetime employment known as the iron rice bowl (铁饭碗). An agent of the state, *danwei* also took care of its employees' welfare—from housing and education to transportation and dining. A sample timetable of a household in an enterprise *danwei* offers a glimpse of the traditional *danwei*: every aspect of life, from work to school and from leisure activities to private matters, all happened within the *danwei* compound.[21]

---

17   Ibid.

18   Ibid.

19   Ibid.

20   E. M. Bjorklund, "The Danwei: Socio-Spatial Characteristics of Work Units in China's Urban Society," *Economic Geography* 62 no. 1 (January 1986): 21, 23.

21   Chai Weiyan et. al, 中国城市的单位透视 (China's Urban Danwei) (Nanjing: Southeast University Press, 2016), 70-73; Andrew G. Walder, Communist Neo-Traditionalism: Work and Authority in Chinese Industry (Berkeley: University of California Press, 1986), 14-27.

Danwei's enclosed nature created what scholars label as an "urban village" or a "society without strangers."[22] This sense of exclusivity and familiarity as well as security and protection fostered a strong collective identity or the "*danwei* complex (单位情结)," best reflected in the popular slogan of "treating *danwei* as family (以单位为家)" or "treating factory as family (以厂为家)."[23] *Danwei* affiliation replaced hometown or locality as the primary source of one's public identity (身份).[24]

Beginning in the 1970s, series of reforms curtailed *danwei*'s influence in the society. Economic reform opened doors for private companies and forced many unprofitable SOEs into bankruptcy and massive layoffs of factory workers, especially in northeastern China. Marketization also dismantled *danwei*'s function as mini welfare states during the pre-reform era. With increasing demand for public provision of social welfare services such as primary education and rudimentary healthcare, schools and clinics, once located within individual *danwei* compounds, became accessible to the general public.

Then came the 1990s and 2000s, a period marked by housing reform and, with it, further deconstruction of the enclosed spatial and social structure of the *danwei* system. The commercialization of the housing market brought new regulations. These regulations, in turn, stripped individual work units of the power to distribute apartments as part of

---

22 Bjorklund, "The Danwei," 21.

23 Chai et. al, *China's Urban Danwei*, 75-76.

24 Li, *Thoughts*, 23.

their welfare packages. Consequently, by 1998, *danwei* had ceased to function as a total institution governing China's urban population.

Radical changes in China significantly curtailed the overwhelming power and influence of work units. Still, the structure of a *danwei* society did not collapse. Despite privatization of most economic activities at the structural level, key social and economic resources—from education and healthcare to energy and finance—remain in the hands of the state. This is especially true in non-first-tiered cities where high quality education and healthcare resources belong to public schools and hospitals. In other words, though the series of reforms since the 1970s weakened the resource allocation power of each individual work unit, the overarching structure of *danwei*, or state-run society, has remained in place.

PUBLIC CAREER AND PRIVATE CITIZENS

At the individual level, the dismantling of *danwei*'s role as a total institution fundamentally changed the employment relationship within the *danwei* system. Marketization ended the era of the *danwei* mini-welfare state. Economic and social changes ushered in a new age of autonomy, opportunity, and uncertainty, replacing the Socialist era of comprehensive welfare and control administered by the total institution. At the same time, however, *danwei* is not reduced to merely a place of work for public servants. For some, benefits once ubiquitous and unextraordinary that survived the reforms have become a special perquisite or privilege only associated with a *danwei* career. The iron rice bowl of lifetime employment, for example, remains untouched by the dramatic social changes, guaranteeing a sense of security and stability unimaginable in the private sector. Moreover, the state's powerful presence fosters a sense of status and social respect for *danwei* employees. Having a career in public service means being part of the system that maintains a strong influence in social and economic activities. In the eyes of many—especially those who experienced the pre-reform era—a stable and respectable career *danwei* position is a symbol of success.

Younger generation Chinese also demonstrate unyielding enthusiasm for a *danwei* career. Against the waning influence and power of the *danwei* system from an individual perspective, its popularity soared exponentially in recent years as millions of young university graduates each year participate in the fierce competition for a *danwei* career. In 2019, over 5.2 million recent college graduates entered the impossible quest for a career in civil service. With less than fifteen thousand available positions nationwide, the overall acceptance rate barely exceeds 2.5 percent.[25] Finding a job in a state-owned institute, though not as competitive, is still against great odds. In Hefei, for example, the most sought-after position in a state-owned institute—exhibition manager in the provincial Innovation Service Center—has 1,305 applicants with only one opening.[26]

When Ms. Zhang applied for her current position, she did not know how many competitors she faced. But recounting

---

25 Data collected from Huatu Education and Zhonggong Education. Civil service exam comprises of national exam and provincial exam.

26 "2019年合肥市市直事业单位最终31816人参加考试 (Hefei State-owned Institute Had 31,816 Applicants Taking Entrance Examination)," Airui Guide, published August 9, 2019.

the intense hiring process she experienced, she said she must have done better than hundreds of other applicants. She passed the writing exam with the highest score and aced subsequent interviews. Upon finishing the application process, Ms. Zhang received her acceptance letter and soon began her career in public service.

Public enthusiasm for a public career, interestingly, has not always been this high since the late 1970s. In the 1980s and 1990s, thousands of young, ambitious *danwei* employees rebelled against the rigidity of a *danwei* career to embrace the liberal spirit and stand at the forefront of economic and political reform. This spirit is perhaps best reflected in two novels written by Liu Zhenyun, *Danwei* and *Yidi Jimao* (一地 鸡毛 *Ground Covered with Chicken Feathers*).[27] Both stories center around the mundane life of a young *danwei* employee, Lin. A recent university graduate with ambitious aspiration, Lin discovered that beneath the congenial façade, *danwei* is a swamp of alliance and betrayal as everyone sought to advance his or her own interests at the expense of others. Struggling to stay away, Lin was ultimately defeated by a series of trivial and mundane conflicts and became a sophisticated player in the game of power like everyone else.

Though written over thirty years ago, the stories Liu depicts remain relatable to thousands of Chinese today. For many, Lin's life—mundane yet full of trivial troubles—is no different from their own. The social environment has changed

27   刘震云 (Liu Zhenyun), 一地鸡毛 (*Ground Covered with Chicken Feathers*) (Wuhan: Changjiang Literature Publishing House, 1993); 刘震云 (Liu Zhenyun), 单位 (*Danwei*) (Wuhan: Changjiang Literature Publishing House, 1988).

dramatically since the 1990s, but the aspiration for a simple but better life has not. People may no longer worry about a pound of soured tofu or a basket of pears, but purchasing an apartment and financing children's education are not lighter burdens. Against this backdrop, the disillusionment felt when such dreams are defeated by reality still resonates with many.

This begs the question: why are Chinese well-educated youth embracing a remnant of the Socialist past rejected by their parents' generation?

To answer this, I set out to conduct a fieldwork project in Hefei in the summer of 2019. To know what drives young college graduates to a career in public service, I first needed to determine whether "successful" *danwei* employees, indeed, live the Chinese Dream. My fieldwork involved interviews and participant observations with entry-level public servants of various government agencies. The selection of civil servants as a sample representing the larger population of *danwei* employees not only reflects the prominence and symbolic nature of civil servants among public employees but also accounts for the fact that many SOEs have introduced a dual-track system distinguishing formal employees from contractual employees, who receive few of the benefits granted to the former and often occupy entry-level positions that I seek to examine.

In this book, I use the concepts "public employees," "civil servants," and "*danwei* employees" interchangeably, as they refer to the same group of people in my case study. Although addressing them as *danwei* employees would more accurately reflect the connotation the term "public servants (公务员)" implies in the Chinese context, my emphasis on using these three terms interchangeably serves two purposes: 1) to familiarize my readers with the uniquely Chinese concept of *danwei*, and 2) to remind my readers that despite all these connotations, at the end of the day, these civil servants should be, both in the literal and legal definitions, people serving the interests of the public.

PART TWO

WELL-TO-DO MIDDLE CLASS

不搞改革开放，只有死路一条

邓小平　1992年南巡

*If we don't pursue Reform and Opening,
we will run into a dead-end.*

DENG XIAOPING DURING THE SOUTHERN TOUR IN 1992

CHAPTER 3

ECONOMIC CAPITAL

I heard a loud cry in the corridor when I walked up the flight of stairs that leads to Mr. Chen's office. It was paycheck day—a day when, I later learned, everyone in the work units receives a long, narrow strip of paper indicating their salaries, taxes, extra fees, bonuses, and a number indicating total income. When I walked into his office, I caught a quick glimpse of Mr. Chen's paycheck on top of his calculator. The final number at last column, including bonuses and deducting tax and insurances, comes out to approximately 5,500 RMB ($810) per month. To put this in comparative terms, a report issued by Zhilian Zhaopin (智联招聘), one of the most authoritative career development platforms in China, stated that by the beginning of 2020 the average monthly salaries at Hefei had reached 8,208 RMB ($1,212).[28] Shocked and bewildered by how much the public sector lags behind the municipal average, I tried my best to hide my expression.

---

28 智联招聘 (Zhaoping), 2020年冬季中国雇主需求与白领人才供给报告 (*Report on Employers Demand and White-Collar Talents Supply in Winter of 2020*) (Beijing: Zhaoping, 2020).

Fortunately, Mr. Chen made no secret of his financial situation. Before I asked my rather awkward question probing into his personal life, Mr. Chen had already begun detailing his experience as a public servant, starting with the paycheck. "The salary of public employees is an art of addition rather than subtraction," he said. Imagine comparing Mr. Chen's salary to a private sector employee earning 10,000 RMB ($1,477) on paper each month. The latter may only bring home, on average, 8,160 RMB ($1,200) per month accounting for year-end bonus after paying 30 percent income taxes. Mr. Chen, on the other hand, can expect to earn 8,250 RMB ($1,220) each month because his paychecks reflect the post-tax salaries and *danwei* usually awards employees with a hefty sum of year-end bonuses worth as much as six months of salaries.

CHINESE URBAN MIDDLE CLASS

With a disposable income of close to those earning 10,000 RMB a month, civil servants in Hefei can enjoy comfortable though not affluent lives. Domestic standards in China define middle-class citizens as those earning between 60,000 RMB ($7,250) to 500,000 RMB ($62,500) a year.[29] McKinsey adopts a similar but slightly narrower range, between 75,000 RMB ($11,500) and 280,000 ($43,000) per year.[30] By either metric, public employees fall comfortably into Chinese middle class. At the same time, however, they have yet to reach the level of prosperity that falls under the category of "new middle

29   China Power Team, "How Well-off is China's Middle Class," China Power, updated October 29, 2020.
30   Ibid.

class (新中产阶级)" put forth by a joint report produced by Jinyuan Investment Group and Hurun Report.

According to this *China New Middle Class Report*, China's new middle class, which accounts for 33 million households in China, describes a well-educated, affluent group of citizens that devote less than 50 percent of their household disposable income on necessary expenditures.[31] By this definition, a new middle class household in China owns at least one real estate property, earn more than 300,000 RMB ($44,370) annually, and have more than 3 million RMB ($443,700) net worth of asset.[32] While this elite category certainly rules out civil servants such as Mr. Chen, the affluence with occasional indulgence of luxury embodied by this group is well beyond the goal of moderate prosperity.

Though not considered a high-paying career path in Hefei, public service promises a more than moderate compensation compared to the municipal average. Surely, the rising Information Technology (IT) industry in Hefei's High-tech Industrial Development Zone (HIDZ) brought new, high-paying employment opportunities, but those belong to the skilled, selective few. A thread of answers posted by Chinese netizens on Zhihu, a website equivalent to Quora, reveals a common perception among Hefei citizens that view 10,000 RMB as a benchmark for comfort. In the words of one respondent, "[one] faces no pressure meeting basic necessities

---

31   Jinyuan Investment Group and Hurun Report, 2018 中国新中产圈层白皮书 (*China New Middle Class Report*) (Shanghai: Hurun Report, 2018), 9.

32   Ibid.

but may find it difficult affording a high-quality lifestyle."[33] Mr. Chen's experience also echoes this commonly held perception. While he faces no pressure signing up for a monthly gym membership or awarding himself with an occasional affordable luxury, Mr. Chen has only achieved what he terms "superficial affluence," for those rare indulgences often precipitate a few weeks, if not months, of intentional frugality by "eating less and walking more."

Those who choose this path do not expect to achieve great wealth. If anything, the modest salary drives many adventurist spirits away from the *danwei*. So, if not wealth, what is in it for Mr. Chen and thousands like him who pursue a life in public service? The short answer is stability.

SECURITY OVER SALARIES

Recounting his reason for becoming a public servant, Mr. Chen made an analogy comparing finding a job in China's saturated labor market to making an investment choice: "it's either a risky path with high return or a stable progression of moderate income." The risky path certainly represents the private sector, where salaries are higher but the chance of demotion, firing, and transfer remain uncertain. The *danwei* system, on the other hand, guarantees lifetime employment with the iron rice bowl to its formal employees, promising a consistent and predictable level of income tied to the rank or professional title.

---

33 Anonymous User, answer to "月薪一万在合肥能过什么样的生活? (What Kind of Lifestyle Can One Afford in Hefei with A Monthly Salary of 10,000 RMB?" Zhihu, updated June 21, 2017.

Mr. Chen realizes his pessimistic view on China's labor market backed by a booming economy and his strong preference for stability over higher rewards seem contradictory, incompatible even, with the general optimism regarding China's rapid GDP growth and the emergence of successful Chinese tech companies led by young entrepreneurs. In his defense, this perceived anomaly only rings true for the fortunate or very successful few, and for Mr. Chen, "the great aspirations and expectations for future lives and career upon graduation…was ultimately defeated by the brutal reality." Many in China shared a similar sense of insecurity and lack of confidence. The 2015 China General Social Survey (CGSS) conducted by Renmin University reveals a clear priority given to stability among Chinese urban citizens as demonstrated in Figure 1. Although younger, more educated respondents are significantly more likely to value criteria such as whether the work is interesting over stability, preference for stability remains very high among this group as well. The lack of differentiation among those who received higher education fails to account for the complexity and sharp disparity among the well-educated youth in China.

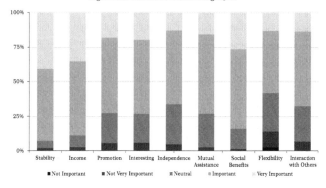

Figure 1. Significant factors for Chinese in job considerations. Data collected from China General Social Survey (CGSS) 2015 and arranged by author. The original survey asks respondents to rank the significance of the nine factors when considering a job from not important (1) to very important (5). The nine factors are: 1) stability (工作稳定); 2) high income (收入高); 3) promotion opportunities (好的升职机会); 4) work is interesting (工作有趣); 5) can work independently (可以让人独立工作); 6) allow mutual assistance (可以让大家互相帮助); 7) beneficial to the society (对社会有益); 8) flexible (可以让人自由决定工作时间或天数); 9) can interact with other people (能够与他人打交道).

In the early 1990s, China implemented several measures to gradually expand university enrollment rate. More than two decades later, a college degree has become so ubiquitous in China that the value of an applicant's college diploma depreciates significantly if it isn't embossed with the name of a top-tier university. Within China's university hierarchy, the C9 League comprising nine world-class universities stand out as an equivalent to the Ivy League in the US. Beneath the C9 are Project 985 and Project 211 colleges designated by the government as research universities. Following these approximately one hundred universities, the rest are further divided into lesser first-tiered, second-tiered, and third-tiered universities.

This hierarchy not only determines the quality of one's higher education, but also his or her career path and future potential post graduation. Many companies in China institute a cutoff line based on undergraduate education, only offering those graduated from Project 211 colleges or above a chance to compete in the interview rounds.

This issue of discrimination based on a rigid standard of education is not a secret to Chinese citizens. Many even believe evaluating an applicant solely considering his or her academic degree is a fair, impartial practice. In 2021, the release of the second season of a reality TV show kindled discussions on the current system. *An Exciting Offer* (令人心动的offer) invites ten recent law school graduates to intern at reputable law firm in Shanghai, Jun He Law Office (君合律师事务所). The film crew documents how these interns overcome challenges to prove they should qualify for the three return offers. In the second season, aired between November 2020 and January 2021, Ding Hui stood out as the oldest intern in the cohort and the only graduate of a non-Project 985 or Project 211 university. Though he also received a reputable law degree from East China University of Political Science and Law, Ding Hui's background remains lackluster in comparison to other interns with extensive study abroad experience at world-class universities such as Georgetown and Stanford.

Ding Hui's difficult path began even before the internship started. During the pre-internship interview section, HR representatives from Jun He questioned Ding Hui why he should be considered given his age and not-so-outstanding undergraduate degree. In later episodes, Ding Hui's diligence earned the sympathy and respect of thousands of viewers but not the approvals of lawyers at Jun He. During one of the earlier challenges, Ding Hui stood out as one of the most hardworking, capable, and punctual interns among his cohort, but four lawyers from Jun He ranked him last because he misspelled the *he* (合) in Jun He with a different character, *he* (和). While the mistake was certainly more than negligible, Ding Hui was certainly no worse than other interns who sent documents to the wrong email address. Compared to Li Jinye who graduated from Georgetown Law and seems perfect in any regard or Wang Xiao who graduated from Stanford Law School and boasts of becoming the "aircraft among Chinese lawyers," Ding Hui was much more relatable. Thus to many viewers, Ding Hui's mishap is not just a distant story on reality TV, but a reflection of their own struggles in the job market.

For Mr. Chen, who graduated from a lesser-known second-tiered university near Hefei, the promise of the education embodied in the ancient wisdoms only belongs to those graduating from Project 211 universities or above. Upon graduation, Mr. Chen soon realized that "everything [he has] fought for during [his] teenage years amounts to nothing in front of a HR officer." As he recounted his disillusionment with education, Mr. Chen mentioned the sensational news that a PhD candidate from Tongji University could only find a job as a sanitation worker. Though the rumor was later disproven, the very idea that one may end up as a sanitation worker, a career many parents in China look down upon as a symbol of "failure," is terrifying enough itself.

The sudden realization that higher education cannot guarantee success shatters the belief of "education changes destiny" that motivated many like Mr. Chen, who had hoped for a bright future after graduation. A sense of defeat and helplessness may overwhelm many recent college graduates, encouraging a more pragmatic and calculated outlook. If higher education can be an empty promise of success, any risk promising great return seems like another deception bearing nothing but fruit of bitterness in the future.

On top of this disillusionment, the current economic climate deters risky undertakings by young people. With living costs, especially housing prices, rising faster than salaries, many recent college graduates are less motivated by the desire to make a difference but by the realistic consideration of becoming a homeowner and securing a comfortable living. Mr. Liu, a colleague and friend of Mr. Chen, explained this dilemma: "The material and psychological rewards of successfully chasing one's dream is certainly enticing, but the cost of failure is simply out of the picture." Trained by reality to be over-calculating and utilitarian, young people today are "zealous and ambitious on their quest for promotion" on the one hand and "fearful of making a wrong judgment or squandering time on useless projects" on the other.

Prioritizing certainty and stability over adventure and rewards, millions of recent graduates diffident of their capability to succeed in the uncertain private sector find the appeal of *danwei*'s iron rice bowl irresistible. After my interview with Mr. Chen, he forwarded me a news article from 2012. The headline immediately caught my attention—"3,000 university graduates compete for janitor positions."[34] The article interviewed a young graduate, Mr. Dong Peng, who failed to land a secure employment six months after graduation.

After switching between several jobs—a can manufacturer at a chemical plant, a security at a pharmaceutical warehouse, and a clerk at an insurance company—Mr. Peng felt he could see no future. An opportunity arrived when his mother brought home the exciting news that government agencies in Harbin are hiring full-time janitors. While a recruitment notice for a sanitation worker typically would not excite the Mr. Peng, the promise of staffing within the *danwei* system caught his attention. Though initially indifferent toward the prospect of becoming a janitor, Mr. Peng was ultimately convinced by his mother. After living in uncertainty for over six months, Mr. Peng finally realized that the only thing he dared to ask for is stability, and if a *danwei* employment could guarantee that, "what is so bad about sweeping the streets?"

The same article also interviewed Mr. Liu Lin, a competitor of Mr. Peng for the janitor position in Harbin who strived for the very same goal of stability. Having worked for the Binxi township government on the outskirt of Harbin as a temporary staff, Mr. Lin enjoyed none of the benefits and security associated with a *danwei* career. For the past two years, he worked on an ad hoc basis, responding to whatever task was assigned by his superior. His status as a temporary rather than a formal staff meant no social security, no

---

34 "哈尔滨3000大学生争考清洁工 称没勇气拒绝 (Over 3,000 College Graduates Compete for A Janitor Post, Claiming that They Do not Have the Courage to Reject)," *Xinhua News*, November 2, 2012.

room for promotion, and no guarantee for monthly salaries: "everyone around me went on with promotion after promotion…with a formal status you can become an official and without one there is no promotion, period. That's the fundamental difference."

Characterized by its hierarchical structure, egalitarianism, and uniformity, the *danwei* system resembles a greenhouse in which employees face no uncertainties. The outside world, in contrast, seems dangerous and unpredictable. Demotion and firing can occur just as easily as promotion and pay raise. The iron rice bowl dispels the fear of tomorrow's unexpected catastrophe. Even during times of shrinking labor demand or economic downturns, "as long as the government does not collapse, you cannot lose your job," says Mr. Peng's mother when convincing her son to apply for the janitor position. Although the position Mr. Peng sought after certainly cannot promise the same level of income enjoyed by desk clerks such as Mr. Chen, as this chapter seeks to demonstrate, material rewards hardly constitute a primary incentive attracting young college graduates to public service.

On top of the guaranteed employment, the equalized pay scale determined by rank and professional title and seldom occurrence of demotion rewards the employees an extra sense of security and predictability. In a labor environment that many such as Mr. Chen consider extremely competitive and even hostile given their less than outstanding resumé, stability far outweighs other concerns. For them, *danwei* is no short of the perfect career path. Within the insular environment where employment and salaries are guaranteed, employees are free from worries of unexpected layoffs, occasional poor performances, or even natural disasters such as the Covid-19 pandemic. In Mr. Chen's words, "if you are willing to sacrifice potential yet slim chance of a high paying job and settle for a guaranteed comfort of moderate prosperity, I see no reason why anyone would not squeeze their way into a *danwei* career."

CHAPTER 4

SOCIAL CAPITAL

———

If foreign friends were to ask me for one important travel tip before visiting China, I would advise them to become familiar with the concept of *guanxi*. There are certainly many things worth mentioning—from where to find the best noodle (it's Shaanxi by the way) to how to communicate with strangers—but I am not alone to stress the importance of *guanxi*. The concept is so crucial to successful business relations in China that international business courses include a *guanxi* component. Loosely translated as relationship, *guanxi* is a social network built upon trust and mutually beneficial relationship.

It is not an exaggeration to say everything in China depends on *guanxi*. When I was preparing to get my driver's license, my mother enrolled me in the driving school where her childhood friend's cousin teaches. My aunt owns a flower shop in Hefei, but if I want to send a bouquet to my girlfriend in Xi'an, I would ask my aunt for the contact of her business partner in Xi'an. Whatever I want to accomplish in China, asking someone within my *guanxi* network for help is always preferable than proceeding without help.

In most instances, these connections are not absolutely necessary but extremely helpful. I could have registered at any reputable driving school driving school in Hefei and pass the test. I can easily search up flower shops in Xi'an and choose one to order a bouquet for my girlfriend. Using my *guanxi* networks may limit my choices, but it makes my experience much easier. I trust people I ask for help because their actions are accountable through our personal connections.

SOCIAL CLASS BEYOND ECONOMICS

How much does personal relationship matter when finding a job? While your answer may depend on personal experience, your estimate may lean toward the lower end given the general social discouragement of nepotism. It will probably come as a surprise that a 2012 research shows 81.6 percent of successful job applicants utilized their social connections during the hiring process; this number has increased significantly from 27.2 percent in the pre-reform era.[35] In the US, Granovetter's research in the 1970s also revealed 57 percent of current employees relied on their personal networks when securing a job position.[36]

What this indicates is not a hidden unjust, nepotistic side of the labor market that favors those with power and connections, but the complexity of class. Economic factors alone fail to capture the complex dynamics of social stratification.

---

35 Bian Yanjie, Zhang Wenhong, and Cheng Cheng, "A Social Network Model of the Job-Search Process: Testing A Relational Effect Hypothesis," *Chinese Journal of Sociology* 32, no. 3 (2012): 32.

36 Mark S. Granovetter, *Getting a Job: A Study of Contacts and Careers* (Chicago: University of Chicago Press, 1974), 33.

Bourdieu's framework emphasizes social capital because social networks also play significant roles in determining one's status within society and generating social cleavages. An entry-level white-collar employee, for example, may earn the same wage as a senior blue-collar worker, but personal connections with wealthy, powerful colleagues may elevate the status of the former. In recent years, this more comprehensive framework of understanding class beyond the mere economic perspective of the Marxist tradition has gained prominence outside theoretical implications.

The BBC class calculator, a new project and experiment launched in 2013, captures the complex and diverse string of ingredients that determine the distinct group of people in which one belongs and associates. The survey inquires into typical economic indicators such as salaries, savings, and house ownership status. It also probes deeper—respondents provide insight into their social networks and cultural tastes. The survey's evaluation of a respondent's social networks bases not only on how diverse his or her connections are, but also the professions of those connections. Having a lawyer friend, for example, is worth higher points than knowing a receptionist. The class calculator finally determines the cultural attainment of respondents by asking their preferred activities, ranging from "[going] to stately homes" and "[socializing] at home" to "[listening to jazz]" and "[watching] dance or ballet."[37] The calculator then places respondents in one of seven categories and expands on the traditional upper, middle, and working-class groupings.

---

37   Paul Kerley, "What is your 21st Century Social Class?" BBC, December 7, 2015.

Whereas the traditional upper class still forms its own group as the elite in the new category, middle and working classes are each further broken down into three different groups with similar economic dispositions but distinct social networks and cultural tastes. New affluent workers, for example, differ from the technical middle class and established middle class as they are typically younger with high scores in emerging culture, while showing fewer interests in highbrow culture, such as classical music and theater. Among the three groups that make up the traditional working class, emergent service workers have much more social and cultural capitals than the traditional working class and precariat—a group of people suffering from a precarious condition without predictability or security—without faring better financially.[38]

GUANXI AND PINDIE

BBC's new model of seven class categories does not apply to China perfectly. The new understanding of class reflected in this experiment, however, can help us understand social stratification outside the British context. Though the term "social capital (*shehui ziben* 社会资本)" is new to China, the idea that one's personal network and connections can behave in the same ways as material assets has its traces deep within the Chinese cultural heritage.[39] In fact, the Sino version of cultural capital, *guanxi*, carries a much richer meaning in Chinese society. The most traditional conceptualization of *guanxi* refers to the web of familial obligations in which the *guanxi* capital is realized through the fulfillment of moral

---

38 Ibid.

39 Lena Y. Zhong, *Communities, Crime and Social Capital in Contemporary China* (London: Routledge, 2008), 75.

obligations and is rationalized in terms of *mianzi* (面子 face).[40] *Mianzi* can thus function as "a social exchange currency" that can be acquired, gifted, or lost and represent to a large extent status, prestige, and social position within society.[41]

Outside the kinship context, *guanxi* can refer to favor exchanges. This model of conceptualization focuses on the instrumentality and utility of an interpersonal connection, including kinship ties, rationalizing relationship as a form of transaction. A more common conceptualization of *guanxi* in China, proposed by Lin Nan, combines the previous two models and defines *guanxi* as "social-exchange networks of asymmetrical transactions."[42] The asymmetrical nature of *guanxi* means that social interactions and exchanges can occur without promise or expectation of reciprocity, though the person on the receiving end of the favor effectively owes the other party a *renqing* (人情 favor) that should be repaid when such an occasion emerges. Without denying the instrumental value and uses of *guanxi*, Lin also emphasizes the sentimental basis of interpersonal relations: "it is the relationship that is valued and maintained, not the value of the favor transacted per se."[43]

40   Bian Yanjie, "Guanxi Capital and Social Eating: Theoretical Models and Empirical Analyses," in *Social Capital: Theory and Research*, ed. Lin Nan, Ronald S Burt, and Karen S Cook (New York: Aldine de Gruyter, 2001), 277-278.

41   P. Christopher Earley, *Face, Harmony, and Social Structure: An Analysis of Organizational Behavior Across Cultures* (Oxford: Oxford University Press, 1997), 67.

42   Lin Nan, *Social Capital: A Theory of Social Structure and Action* (Cambridge: Cambridge University Press, 2001), 122.

43   Ibid.

Scholars often describe *guanxi* as a Chinese equivalent or expression of social capital, but many acknowledge the complexity of *guanxi* that expands beyond the Western understanding of social capital. Though not formally theorized, *guanxi* embodies the benefits of strong personal ties among individuals prevalent in studies on social capital as well as the strengths of weak social ties among acquaintances. In fact, *guanxi* had become so sophisticated in contemporary China that "it has been elevated to *guanxi-xue* (关系学 the art of *guanxi* studies)."[44] However, the air of erudition evoked by the name "*guanxi-xue*" does little to mask the negative connotation it carries. The term "*xue*" or "art" satirically ridicules the extreme use of *guanxi* as an instrument to achieve selfish ends.[45] Moral condemnation of behaviors such as "going through the back door (*zouhoumen* 走后门)" reflects the ready popular conception that *guanxi* can easily be abused and corrupted for personal gains. Public malfeasance, shady deals between business leaders and government officials, and cronyism all exemplify dishonest and morally detestable use of *guanxi* widely condemned in China.

Concurrent with the severe denunciation of *guanxi* exploitation is a sense of appreciation as it serves as "an important lubricant and propeller" in the Chinese society, in Mr. Huang's words. A key symbol of the ubiquitous and significance of *guanxi* in contemporary China is the *pindie wenhua* (拼爹文化), which translates to the "culture of competing using one's father." The perquisites enjoyed by the sons and daughters of wealthy business owners and high-level officials

---

44 Mayfair Mei-hui Yang, *Gifts, Favors, and Banquets: The Art of Social Relationships in China* (Ithaca: Cornell University Press, 1994), 8.

45 Ibid.

further devalued the significance of education performance, replacing the popular reform era saying "With a good command of mathematics, physics, and chemistry, one may venture to anywhere in the world without fear (学好数理化，走遍天下都不怕)" with the new adage of "A good command of mathematics, physics, and chemistry is not worth as much as having a good father (学好数理化，不如有个好爸爸)."

The prevalence of nepotism and morally condemnable exploitation of *guanxi*—both at the highest level among government leaders and business tycoons as well as the more local level—has changed people's perceptions on the role of *guanxi* within society. Though still regarded as unethical and corrupt, abusive uses of *guanxi* by the rich and powerful elites in society have established themselves as a new norm, commanding jealousy and emulation rather than criticism and condemnation. The ubiquity of this *pindie* culture is best reflected in the nefarious Li Gang incident in 2010.[46]

On October 16, Li Qiming, a student at Hebei University, hit two other university students while drunk driving down a narrow lane on campus. One of the victims died due to injuries sustained in the accident. The other victim was later discharged from hospital but suffered from a broken leg. Without getting out of the car to check on his two classmates, Li fled the scene. He continued driving toward the girls' dormitory at the end of the narrow road and dropped off his girlfriend. When later apprehended by campus police, Li showed little remorse. Instead, he shouted, "Go ahead. I

---

46 "河北大学撞人案疑犯涉交通肇事罪被刑拘 (Suspect Involved in the Hebei University Homicide Detained)," The Beijing News, October 19, 2010.

dare you. Sue me. My dad is Li Gang," believing his father's government position would grant him immunity.[47]

The incident immediately caused an internet outrage. Netizens soon discovered Li Gang's identity, deputy director of the local public security bureau, and Li Qiming's famous "My dad is Li Gang (我爸是李刚)" became a catchphrase and internet meme.

Li Qiming naively believed his father's position would free him from prison. This belief, however, is not so irrational in China. Had Li Qiming been the son of a high-ranking official in Beijing, the incident might have remained hidden from the public and Li Qiming could have walked away without punishment. Abuse of personal connections among top officials controlling the country's political and economic lifelines has long been an open secret in China. This incident, however, revealed the *pindie* culture does not exist among the powerful elites. If someone of Li Gang's rank can embolden his son to commit murder and assume immunity, how many more are exploiting their close ties with rich and powerful figures within society?

The incident also indirectly reflects the power and prestige of a *danwei* career. The state's monopoly over key resources for governance means that work units in charge of fulfilling these functions have immense, unchallenged power. In Li Qiming's defense, his father had considerable power as the deputy director of the municipal police department. Had the incident remained a local affair, Li Gang could have offered

---

47   Ibid.

his son some protection or even a "get out of jail free" card. Unfortunately for Li Qiming, his naive hope vanished as soon as his hit-and-run went viral on the internet. The court found him guilty and sentenced him a six-year sentence. In less extreme cases, sons of a director of the education department face no obstacle enrolling in the best schools in the city and daughters of officials in leadership positions can expect secure career paths arranged by their parents.

SMALL FAVORS AND POWERFUL PRESTIGE

Exploiting close ties with rich and powerful figures for personal gains is a common practice for those with valuable connections. Rarely do they play a decisive role in the considerations and calculations of the grassroots level *danwei* employees. Some, including Mr. Chen and Mr. Liu, hope to find their way to leadership positions by mid-career, but they largely express disdain rather than admiration toward the abusive practices. Instead, for most of them, being in a *danwei* itself offers a different form of social capital that resembles the weak ties in Granovetter's thesis.[48]

Unlike strong social ties such as kinship, weak ties refer to connections with acquaintances and colleagues—people we know but only to a limited extent. People sharing weak ties may not have similar hobbies, come from similar backgrounds, or spend leisure time together, but these connections have their advantages. Whereas networks of strong ties often form small, enclosed loops, networks of weak social ties

---

48   Mark S. Granovetter, "The Strength of Weak Ties," *American Journal of Sociology* 78, no. 6 (May 1973): 1260-1380.

are expansive and limitless. One likely will not entrust their lives and assets to a mere acquaintance, but he or she may ask a colleague or distant friend for less demanding requests. Because one's weak-ties network tends to be more diverse, the likelihood that someone can be of assistance is significantly higher than within the small network of strong ties.

When I asked most of my interviewees whether they benefited from the social ties cultivated through their *danwei*, almost all responded affirmatively. Many, however, struggled to provide any specific example. Mr. Dong, after half a minute of silence and glancing around his office, responded apologetically, "Sorry I couldn't give you anything useful. They are really small things, you know, and don't really require any trouble for the other party…just small favors."

Mr. Zhou mentioned how his connection with an employee at the municipal airport did him a simple yet miraculous favor. When sending his two daughters to the US for college for the first time, Mr. Zhou could only accompany them to the security checkpoint. Worried the heavy luggage would cause potential trouble, Mr. Zhou requested an acquaintance he met through work to look after his daughters until they boarded. Recalling the sense of calm after hearing his daughters were safely escorted to the boarding gate, Mr. Zhou commented on how small favors through mere acquaintances are no less powerful than asking a close friend or family members for help.

When asked whether the favor would have been possible had he not been working in his current *danwei*, Mr. Zhou paused for a second and said, "Well, if I hadn't worked for my *danwei*

I wouldn't have known the person. I guess you can say I don't need to be in a *danwei* to know him, but it certainly helps."

Certainly, *guanxi* is not exclusive to *danwei* employees, but *danwei* confers several advantages and privileges not enjoyed by those outside the system. First, as the state controls and governs key public resources, knowing the right person in the relevant *danwei* can open doors otherwise closed or invisible. While personal relationships can be cultivated through kinship and friendship, the workplace offers the best opportunity to expand one's network by far. As most strong personal ties such as family and close friends are limited in number and tend to create small, insulated circles, weak ties established in the workplace can present new opportunities. From this perspective, *danwei* places its employees in more advantageous positions to expand their network that will one day benefit them in times of need.

In Fei Xiaotong's "ripple" model (*chaxu geju* 差序格局) of social structure, Chinese society is best represented by the ripples emerging from the splash of a rock into the water: "Everyone stands at the center of the circles produced by his or her own social influence. Everyone's circles are interrelated. One touches different circles at different times and places."[49] This model suggests relationships in China are without distinct boundaries and can be cultivated and created. For a *danwei* employee, the potential *guanxi* he or she can cultivate from existing networks of colleagues may provide as many as, if not more, opportunities than kinship connections. The

---

49 Fei Xiaotong, From the Soil: The Foundations of Chinese Society (Berkeley: University of California Press, 1992), 62-63.

effectiveness of a secondary and even tertiary connection is notably strong within the *danwei* context. With only a tenuous tie between two strangers, a shared *danwei* background can serve as a foundation of mutual trust. In Mr. Chen's words, "By being in a *danwei* you automatically have a sign of approval. Wherever you go, just say what *danwei* you are from and people will trust you because of your *danwei*."

Greater opportunities to cultivate social ties within the *danwei* system also offer *danwei* employees an invisible form of social capital deriving from the potential of a valuable relationship. While it seems counterintuitive for a not yet materialized connection to carry any weight in society, in practice the power of the invisible *guanxi* has often taken for granted. When asked to recount an example of benefits and privilege received from her *guanxi* cultivated through the *danwei*, Mrs. Chen told me a story of her recent triumph over the inefficient bureaucracy. She convinced a clerk at the municipal exit and entry administration department to break the rules for her son, whose request to renew his passport was initially rejected.

When Mrs. Chen accompanied her son to renew his passport, she was unaware the government only allows citizens to renew their passports one year before expiration. She first tried to convince the clerk handling the passport renewal service that her son may remain overseas for more than ten months so upon his next return an expired passport may cause unnecessary trouble. The clerk, unmoved by the explanation, insisted they find an alternative solution. Annoyed by the staff's indifferent and arrogant remarks, Mrs. Chen demanded to see his immediate superior for consultation. Shocked by her unusual request, the clerk fought back.

"He asked me, 'Who do you think you are?'" Mrs. Chen crossed her arms and spoke in a deep voice, imitating the clerk. "So I responded, 'You don't need to know who I am, just get me your superior!'"

"Then what happened?" I pressed on.

"Well, he certainly seemed frightened by my words and did what I initially asked for. After all, everyone lives under someone else," said Mrs. Chen.

I wondered whether Mrs. Chen had been scared throughout the incident. "Why should I be?" She shook her head, "He was the one being unreasonable. Someone like him should be yelled at for not serving the people."

What surprised me was that when Mrs. Chen asked to see the clerk's superior, she did not have a plan in mind. "I don't have any *guanxi* inside that department, but why does it matter? I'm in a *danwei*, I can easily find my way to establish a *guanxi* with someone in there. Plus, I've worked in a *danwei* for decades—I know his cards. He may scare a regular citizen but not a *danwei* employee like me."

In Mrs. Chen's case, the absence of tangible *guanxi* did not hamper her from effectively harnessing her social capital. While not all forms of *guanxi* exist exclusively within the *danwei* system and the private sector can facilitate the cultivation of different social networks not so readily available to *danwei* employees, having *guanxi* inside the *danwei* is synonymous with having connections within the government. As the state maintains its decisive role in economic planning, political governance, and resource allocation, a solid *danwei* network is as valuable as financial assets. Oftentimes, "money alone can't solve your problem, you need *guanxi* and money... and sometimes when your favor is not that big, *guanxi* alone can get you things money can't buy," according to Mrs. Chen.

Like the construction of social class, the appeal of a *danwei* career is not purely economic. Work units create an environment that facilitates their employees' accumulation of social capital vertically within their *danwei* and horizontally across different work units. Even for those who do not explicitly make expanding their networks a priority, their connections are no less valuable. Once inside a *danwei*, many doors open if you are willing to give them a push. *Danwei* employees are part of a larger web of *guanxi* purely because of their workplace. *Danwei* and *guanxi* work on a basis of mutual trust and symbolic status, which oftentimes leads to advantageous relationships. As Mr. Chen says, "It is not just whom you know that matters, but also whom you may know through those you know already."

CHAPTER 5

STATUS AND PRESTIGE

——

Right around the time of month when pay slips arrive and mortgage is due, Mr. Chen's feeling of ambivalence returns. He sometimes questions the choice he made long ago to pursue a *danwei* career and the meager salary that comes with it. Most of the time, however, he remains proud of his profession. "[Being in a *danwei*] rewards me with a sense of recognition from family and friends…though it has no inherent exchange value, it has psychological benefits by making me proud and confident of myself, especially when compared to my peers."

Decades since the abolition of the work unit system, arguing that *danwei* employees have high social status seems like an outdated assertion. While elites in politics are well respected, low-level public servants whose salaries can only satisfy necessities for a comfortable lifestyle garner much less respect. In comparison, even entry-level employees at foreign enterprises such as IBM or famous domestic corporations such as Alibaba command greater respect. Such a statement, however, reflects a prevalent mentality only among China's upper-middle class, especially in highly developed metropolises such as Shanghai and Shenzhen. When we move down the social ladder to talk about middle-class citizens in China who are not well endowed with economic and social capital, the status of a *danwei* career becomes conspicuous.

The intense competition and high volatility in the labor market have convinced many middle-class parents that *danwei* is a better home for their children than the uncertain private sector. Mr. Huang, for example, confided that he would like his son to secure a comfortable job in a good *danwei*. When I poke for more details about his son, Mr. Huang told me about his son, Huang Ke. He also shared his feeling that he has the obligation to provide at least guidance, if not direct assistance, in Huang Ke's post-graduation future.

After finishing his bachelor's degree in a lesser-known third-tiered university in Changzhou, Huang Ke was lost with what to do after college. With the serendipity of a personal connection through his father's high school classmate and his own hard work, Ke received an offer for a master's program in the New Media Department at the University of Science and Technology of China (USTC), one of the best universities in China and a member of the C9 League. On track to graduate within a year after my interview with Mr. Huang during the summer of 2019, Ke did not have a concrete plan about what to do after acquiring his master's degree. As graduation nears, Mr. Huang grew more anxious about his son's future.

Puzzled by the hinted pessimism, I asked, "Graduating from USTC is a sterling achievement. Why do you worry about his future?"

Mr. Huang paused for a moment and sighed. "Surely it is. But a master's from a good university is worth much less than a bachelor's degree. On top of that, new media is not necessarily one of the disciplines such as computer science that almost guarantee you a job after graduation."

Having spent his entire career in the organizational department, Mr. Huang knows the ins and outs of the *danwei* system. "It is certainly not well paid, but it gives you security and status. And that status is convincing millions of young college graduates to compete for limited spots."

Mr. Huang is certainly not alone in his belief that the status given to *danwei* employees commands respect and prestige in Chinese society. Mr. Chen maintains that though this sense of status and accomplishment provides more psychological benefits than material, the manifestation of such a status becomes tangible in the marriage and dating market. For both men and women looking for a suitable partner, status as a *danwei* employee is a noticeable bonus and sometimes even a preferable asset.

IDEAL BACHELOR AND RELIABLE PARTNER

Economic and social privatization and marketization have significantly liberalized the private sphere within the past few decades. Though inertia to the freedom of love still exists—from the censure on *zaolian* (早恋 puppy love) to the taboo topic related to intimate relationships—young people are usually free to choose whom they date and fall in love with. The freedom to choose who to date and marry, however, rarely includes the freedom to opt out of dating and marriage.

Most single Chinese citizens in their twenties and thirties face constant pressure from their parents to find a date, get married, and have children. The trend of postponing marriage and declining birth rate intensifies widespread anxiety among parents, who fear their children, especially daughters, will die in solitude (孤独终老).[50]

This fear and anxiety has led to the growing popularity of a new term, *shengnv* (剩女), which literally translates as "leftover women." The neologism first came under the spotlight in 2007 when state-run media in China started using this term. That same year, the word *shengnv* was added to the official dictionary under the definition of "well-educated, high-income women who cannot find ideal marriage arrangements after 27."[51] In the same year, All-China Women's Federation published a series of articles stigmatizing "leftover women." In a lengthy article titled "Leftover Women Do Not Deserve Our Sympathy," the author argues that

> *Pretty girls do not need a lot of education to marry into a rich and powerful family. But girls with an average or ugly appearance will find it difficult. These girls try to make themselves more competitive by getting higher degrees, but sadly, they never realize the value of a woman depreciates with age. When they receive their*

---

50 The gender difference in the marriage market will be further explored in the next part dedicated to various topics on gender stratification in China.

51 Research Group for The Language Situation in China, 中国语言生活状况报 2006 (*The Language Situation in China 2006*) (Beijing: Commercial Press, 2007).

master's and doctor's degree, they have only become old and worthless.[52]

Derogatory uses of *shengnv* soon faced severe backlashes from urban, young women, many of whom happily chose the single life. However, single, well-educated young women capable of supporting themselves still face constant pressure to find someone and get married. While many individuals, especially women, view China's growing "leftover women" population positively, negative social comments are far from scarce. Common negative labels on *shengnv* include "material (物质)," "need to be saved (拯救)," "troublesome (麻烦)," "captious (挑剔)," and "vane (虚荣)."[53]

Parents have responded to this crisis by playing a more active role in deciding the future of their children, shifting the largely private matter of love and marriage to the public sphere. In the early 2010s, matchmaking (相亲) shows mushroomed across different TV channels in China. The most successful and popular one—*If You Are the One*(非诚勿扰)—invites twenty-four female guests on stage to decide whether they want to date the rotating male guests, based on three video clips on their personal information and friends' recommendations. Demand for originality in the matchmaking reality shows has continued to rise. Many producers realized simply emulating Western matchmaking shows failed

52 The article has hence been removed, but for citation of this, see Peter Simpson, "The 'Leftover' Women: China Defines Official Age for Females Being Left on the Shelf as 27," *Daily Mail*, February 21, 2013.

53 Zong Zhiyuan et al, 她，为什么'剩下'？——2016 中国城市"剩女"问题大数据研究报告 (*Why Is She Leftover? 2016 Urban China "Leftover Women" Research Report*) (Guangdong: Yangcheng Evening News, 2016), 21-22.

to mobilize many potential viewers eager for more Chinese elements. Many channels have hence touted the new "Chinese style matchmaking (中国式相亲)," inviting parents on stage and shifting the focus from dating (恋) to marriage (婚).

Traditional word of mouth channels that connect individuals within relatively close social circles no longer serve the goal sufficiently and efficiently. Anxious parents are exploring new ways to advertise their still unmarried children in the marriage market. Throughout Chinese cities, matchmaking corners (相亲角) organized by parents have sprouted as online dating apps gain wide popularity. Always based in the most popular park in each city—the People's Park (人民公园) in Shanghai and the Apricot Garden (杏花公园) in Hefei—these matchmaking corners fostered a new norm of "park matchmaking (公园相亲)" in which singles looking for a match are commercialized. Love, an essence of a successful marriage, is a luxury. Tangible attributes and arbitrary qualities such as height, income, amicableness, and willingness to take care of family are prioritized whereas personalities and hobbies are downplayed and ignored.[54]

Only 22 percent of men and 9 percent of women mentioned hobbies in their self-advertisement posters in Shanghai's matchmaking corner.[55] The gender gap derives largely from frequent mentions of "having no bad hobbies" such as smoking, drinking, and gambling among male respondents. Similarly, personality descriptions were also highly

---

54 "我们去了相亲角6次，收集了这874份征婚启事 (We Went to Matchmaking Corner Six Times and Collected 874 Marriage Posters)," *The Paper*, August 17, 2018.

55 Ibid.

homogenous, with men favoring words such as "responsible (负责)," "bright (阳光)," and "prudent (稳重)," and women preferring descriptors such as "kind (善良)," "poised (大方)," and "gentle (温柔)."[56]

In this world of matchmaking run by parents, a *danwei* career symbolizing stability is a treasured attribute. Though few flyers list "having a *danwei* career" as a required quality for a desirable match, being a *danwei* employee automatically checks many boxes of desirable attributes such as economic stability, trustworthiness, and devotion to family. One certainly does not need to be a public servant to be stable, honest, and caring, and not all *danwei* employees are ideal partners. But in eyes of many, the state serves as a reliable screening institution, so anyone approved *danwei* should be a decent, honest person. The stable, predictable employment of a career in public service further promotes the positive image of a *danwei* employee in front of the family of a potential match.[57]

PRESTIGIOUS PUBLIC SERVICE

Why do Chinese people attribute great respect to public employees?

Rapid economic growth has redefined success on the basis of economic wealth. Employees of foreign corporations and successful domestic conglomerates especially in the technology industry thus command greater respect than their peers in other professions. For most middle-class citizens, however,

---

56 Ibid.
57 Ibid.

public service, a path rarely associated with wealth, remains a prestigious career. This stems largely from the stability and predictability of a *danwei* career, which is becoming more valuable and attractive amidst recent economic slowdown.

The intense competition in the labor market and rapidly rising costs of living fostered a new wave of pessimism known as the *sang* (丧) culture—a mentality characterized by a reduced work ethic, lack of self-motivation, and apathy toward the traditional definition of success.[58] Though, as Zeng Yuli points out, the *sang* culture does not imply an indifference to success among those that identify with the sentiment, rather, young people "describe themselves as *sang* because they feel that it is futile to pursue traditional notions of success"—such as homeownership and accumulation of personal wealth.[59]

"The student, having completed his learning, should apply himself to be a business person (学而优则商)." Until the late 2000s, this famous reform era quote has defined the pursuit of millions of young people in China. A wordplay on Confucian doctrine stating students should apply themselves to a career of service intellectuals, the slogan reflects the booming economic opportunities of the early reform era. This enthusiasm, however, has now been replaced by the conservative mentality of self-preservation within the *sang* culture. Unable to attain the traditional definition of success, many middle-class youths in China are opting for a new, more achievable standard that emphasizes security rather than wealth

---

58   Zeng Yuli, "Turn Off, Drop Out: Why Young Chinese Are Abandoning Ambition," Six Tone, published July 27, 2017.
59   Ibid.

accumulation. This new youth culture is reinforced by the mentality shared by many senior members of Chinese society who witnessed China's transformation from an impoverished country to a modern miracle. As China achieved modernization and industrialization in an extremely short span of time, social and economic transformations have outpaced attitudinal change within each generation of Chinese citizens. In Mr. Huang's words, "Economic takeoff has only been here for a few decades…for many people, security and stability still take priority."

Influenced by the renewed emphasis on stability rather than adventurous and entrepreneurial spirit, *danwei* is a term synonymous with stability and even rigidity in China, becoming the new symbol of success for many Chinese middle-class citizens. The guaranteed economic security and other added benefits mentioned in previous sections give *danwei* employees, even those at the entry level, a renewed status of respect and social recognition that harkens back to the pre-reform era during which the public sector attracted all the elites within society.

Popular respect for the public sector in China also has embedded cultural logic. The Confucian notion of success for an individual is embodied in the concept of *shi* (士), which often translates to government officials. Though the concept of *shi* embodies more than its literal meaning, the roadmap of "cultivate one's person, regulate one's family, order one's state, and bring peace and tranquility to all (修身, 齐家, 治国, 平天下)" for Chinese intellectuals spelled out their ultimate goal—serving the public. This traditional notion fostered a psychological complex of "official standard (官本位)" that reveres officialdom as a sign of accomplishment and expertise. Though objectively *danwei* no longer employs the cream of the crop of society and the calling of politics as a vocation of intellectuals is long gone in China, the official standard complex remains inveterate in the mentality of many who hope to move up the social ladder: "no matter who you are, becoming an official will bring honor to your ancestors," in the words of Mr. Huang.

Driven by this idea that officialdom signifies prestige and expertise within the Chinese societies, many successful businesspeople are finding their ways into the government shortly before they retire. Mr. Huang maintains many of them are upper-level managers of state-owned enterprises (SOEs) with deep and personal connections with the government apparatus. "They don't really care what government position they get before retiring, since they are only there to fulfill their bucket list." Few entry-level *danwei* employees dream to advance to the level those SOE CEOs can secure for themselves through connections, but one does not need to be a provincial level or higher official to command respect. Talented and ambitious college graduates can climb up to the municipal level by their mid to late careers. At this level, most officials are successful within the system and well respected by those around them.

PART THREE

ILLUSION OF PROSPERITY

正确处理各种社会矛盾……是实现全面
建设小康社会宏伟目标的重要前提

胡锦涛 2005年对省部级主要领导干部讲话

Correctly resolving social contradictions and social tensions...is an important step toward the goal of fully constructing a moderately prosperous society.

HU JINTAO WHEN SPEAKING TO
SENIOR OFFICIALS IN 2005

CHAPTER 6

PARADOX OF PROSPERITY

—

I had a rather paradoxical understanding of this unique career path based on my interactions with my mother. As a public servant, my mother has a job that others envy—few responsibilities, stable salaries, and high social status. As a public servant, my mother also receives a salary so modest that—in her words—it is more "ceremonial." As the son of a public servant, these paradoxical truths informed my understanding of a public service career.

Public servants like my mother are not impoverished, but neither are they in a comfortable, let alone wealthy, position financially. On the day I met and interviewed Mr. Chen, his praises for the economic securities of a *danwei* career were only as significant as his criticism against his underprivileged economic status. For him, this sense of self-perceived disadvantage stems from the lack of financial freedom and the expectation for greater economic rewards.

To an outside observer, Mr. Chen is advancing steadily along the path toward conventional success. He has a stable job in a respectable *danwei*. He owns real estate assets—an apartment complex worth 1.4 million RMB ($205,000).[60] By any Chinese mother's standards, he is only one step short of success. A happy life awaits Mr. Chen once he meets his future wife.

Up close, however, Mr. Chen struggles to maintain his moderately prosperous lifestyle. The pressure to advance along the path led him to invest in real estate he couldn't really afford on a public servant's salary. He confided in me that he could never have afforded the down payment without the largesse of his parents. "I certainly want to be independent and not spend my parents' retirement funds, but how can anyone expect someone like me to buy a house with my salaries and savings?"

Mr. Chen also worries about the mortgages that will surely wipe clean his monthly savings with his current salaries. Mocking himself as a "*fangnu* (房奴)" or "house mortgage slave," a popular term among Chinese youth describing the situation where mortgage significantly restricts one's financial freedom, Mr. Chen sees himself tied down by his new apartment for the next few decades.

---

60   Mr. Chen's apartment cost approximately 17,500 RMB/m2 ($240/ft2) at the time of purchase.

INDEBTED MIDDLE-CLASS HOMEOWNERS

Mr. Chen's worries about his financial situation are common concerns shared by Chinese youth. While the purchasing power of an average Chinese citizen has increased significantly since the late 1970s, the housing market boom has far outpaced salary increases. Rapid urbanization during the reform era transformed China's demographic landscape. Housing demand in China boomed in the 2000s, and this drove housing prices through the roof. To finance their new apartments, homeowners took out hefty loans to secure down payments. By the late 2000s, *fangnu* had advanced from a joke among friends to a hot topic in Chinese pop culture. *Dwelling Narrowness* (蜗居), a popular drama, reflected popular discontent of high housing prices in China. An opinion piece published on *People's Daily* in 2012 summarizes the reality of *fangnu*: "Some strive to become *fangnu*; some feel fortunate to be a *fangnu*, some overdraw their youth and dream to become one, and some overdraw their parents' carefree post-retirement years at the same time."[61]

Since the early 2010s, complaints of high housing prices have incited debates of future trajectories. Some netizens have advocated for becoming a *fangnu* sooner than later to lock in the best price possible. Others have commented high demand for apartments will ultimately decrease and the housing market will fall significantly. For many young people, however, even those who once staunchly stood against becoming mortgage slaves, pressure from family, friends, and society soon became unbearable.

---

61 "房奴必须付出的代价: 透支青春和父母的晚年 (The Price Mortgage Slaves Must Pay: Overdrawing Their Youth and Their Parent's Post-Retirement Years)," *People's Daily*, December 3, 2012.

In the *People's Daily* article, Mr. Guo Dongcai, a recent homeowner in 2012, documented his transformation from a fierce opponent of his *fangnu* colleagues to one himself. For most Chinese, owning a place to live is a matter of principle. Though the size, location, and conditions matter, homeownership is viewed as a necessary criterion of a "capable young man (有为青年)." More importantly, for young men like Mr. Guo, the pressure becomes increasingly significant as they approach their late twenties when marriage comes onto the table.[62]

In China, the significance of homeownership extends far beyond investment in real estate or a symbol of independence and serves as a representation of status. Since the 1970s, the term "Three Big Things (三大件)" has been widely used to denote three symbols of material success and has played significant roles in the marriage market. Over the past five decades, the "Three Big Things" have evolved from a watch, a bicycle, and a sewing machine in the 1970s, a refrigerator, a color television, and a washing machine in the 1980s, and an air conditioner, a personal computer, and a videocassette recorder in the 1990s to an apartment, a car, and money in the twenty-first century. At the same time, the "Three Big Things" also evolved from an aspiration to a prerequisite in marriage, fueling the vicious cycle of high demand and high prices for the housing market.

Almost a decade after Mr. Guo's lament of becoming a *fangnu*, the cost of homeownership remains out of reach. In 2015, a survey conducted by China's central bank, the People's Bank

---

62 Ibid.

of China, revealed that 52 percent of respondents labeled China's housing price as "unacceptably high (高，难以接受)" whereas only 3.8 percent characterized it as "satisfying (令人满意)."[63] Regarding future trajectories, opinions were fairly even, with 15.2 percent predicting a decrease and 18.4 percent saying continual rise.[64]

In the end, that 18.4 percent got it right. Throughout the 2010s, the housing market boom penetrated further west inland. Housing prices rose dramatically in many second- and third-tiered cities, outpacing the increasing purchasing power of China's urban residents. In Hefei, for example, average housing prices increased from 3,748 RMB per square meter ($53.73 per square foot) to 18,516 RMB per square meter ($265.43 per square foot) between 2008 and 2020.[65]

Housing price to income ratio—a better indicator of affordability—tells an equally concerning story. In 2019, China's housing price to income ratio stood at 29.09, the second highest among ninety-three countries surveyed, trailing only Hong Kong, which has been facing serious housing problems given its high population density.[66] Meanwhile, the US has a housing price to income ratio of 3.58.[67]

---

63   Chen Yang, "央行调查报告：52%居民认为房价高 (Central Bank Survey Report: 52% of Residents Think Housing Price Too High)," *The Beijing News*, December 25, 2015.

64   Ibid.

65   "十二年蝶变！合肥房价究竟涨了多少？ (Dramatic Change in 12 Years. How Much Did Housing Prices in Hefei Increase?)," Xin'an Real Estate, published December 17, 2020.

66   "Property Prices Index by Country 2019," Numbeo, accessed January 16, 2021.

67   Ibid.

As China proposes new monetary policies, debates regarding the future of the national housing market. Regardless of one's take on the imminent future of China's real estate bubble, the fact is that many young people in China are in no financial condition to own an apartment without assistance from their parents.

Mr. Liu, a friend of Mr. Chen, harbors an even more pessimistic view toward the economic prospect of his *danwei* career. Both friends eventually arrived at the same career destination, but they travelled very different routes. Mr. Liu lacks the financial support the Chens were able to provide to their sons. After graduation, he worked as a village official before passing the provincial public service exam in 2017. Despite his strong capability within the government and aspiration to advance through the ranks, his arduous economic conditions hardly match his respected status and positive social images. Supporting a family of three with a monthly income of no more than 7,500 RMB ($1,100), the rosy promise of a *danwei* career seems rather a specious deception dissembling the widening gaps of economic inequality:

> With 7,500 RMB each month I can only afford an apartment in my local town and drive over 30 miles to work... without an apartment in the city, I can't give my child a good education...any apartment near my danwei costs more than 22,000 RMB per square meter. How can I ever afford such an expensive place to live? Now I look back, being in a danwei only sounds good to other people. What's the use of it?

More senior members in the *danwei* systems often grapple with similar financial troubles, albeit in different forms and in a more moderate fashion. Unlike the younger generation of *danwei* employees who passed the extremely competitive selection process for a coveted entry-level position, most senior members within the system received their job assignments upon graduating from college. In a time when a college degree was scarce and economic reform has yet to challenge *danwei*'s dominant role in daily economic activities, a *danwei* career embodied economic, social, and political status and privilege unavailable to outsiders. Before many material benefits associated with a *danwei* career, from appealing salaries to housing allocations, disappeared in the 1990s, those who secured a position benefited tremendously. Many senior *danwei* employees thus never shared the same fear so frequently occupying the minds of their younger colleagues. This difference is extremely significant as homeownership is not only a necessary step on the path of success but also a key indicator of living a life of moderate prosperity. Instead, their worries and anxieties center on expenses on children and healthcare.

For *danwei* employees such as Mr. Huang who is in his mid-fifties, mortgages are far from his primary financial worries. While theoretically he had accumulated enough savings to lead a very comfortable lifestyle, Mr. Huang is not free from anxieties. As Mr. Huang's son, Huang Ke, was due to graduate from graduate school in less than a year during the time of our conversation, Mr. Huang cannot help but worry about his son's future—what job will he find, whom he will marry, and where he will buy an apartment. Similar to how Mr. Chen's parents provided him with the down payment to his apartment, Mr. Huang expects himself to do the same for Huang Ke. Regardless of where Huang Ke wants to live and work in the future, an apartment down payment is nothing short of a heavy financial burden on the Huang family.

A FAREWELL TO WEALTH?

A recurring and prevalent sense of restriction on financial freedom constrains not only public servants but many more citizens in China with similar levels of salaries. What sets *danwei* employees apart is their particular dissatisfaction with their compensations when compared to their equally, if not less, qualified counterparts in the private sector. Though earning higher disposable incomes than the municipal average, public servants believe they should be closer to successful managers, not blue-collar workers. Instead, younger *danwei* employees frequently complained about former classmates who are less smart yet more capable of earning much more. In Mr. Dong's words, "if we sit through the same classes, received similar grades, and even shared the same dorm during our teenage years, why should you earn so much more than I do?"

During Mr. Chen's eloquent case listing both the advantages and disadvantages of a public service career, insufficient compensation ("钱少") stood out as his strongest dissatisfaction. Though one ultimately "gets used to it" in Mr. Chen's experience, the weakened consumption capability nevertheless troubles him. Driven by consumption desires reinforced by China's booming e-commerce market, many young people in China are barely saving a penny at the end of the month. Continuing with his criticism, Mr. Chen made an unexpected statement when he challenged the traditional wisdom of "升官发财 (getting promotion in government and getting rich)" with his own saying of "想发财就不要想当官 (if you want to be rich, don't become an official)."

Public opinion, however, reflects sentiments that disprove Mr. Chen's claim. The 2015 China General Social Survey reveals that when asked to select which group of individuals among farmers, blue-collar workers, government officials, company managers, highly skilled and well-educated individuals, and wealthy asset holders have benefited most within the past two decades, 36.85 percent of respondents chose government officials. Asset holders and managers ranked second and third, occupying 24.45 percent and 19.46 percent of the total share respectively.[68] Moreover, what made Mr. Chen's saying especially questionable are publicized cases of low-level government officials accumulating an unfathomable amount of money through corruption.

In the past two decades, many low-ranking officials only one or two levels senior to Mr. Chen have been sentenced to imprisonment, sometimes for life, for corruption and various other felonies. Many of these officials earn similar amounts of salaries as Mr. Chen does on the book, but that is not the end of the story. Abusing their power as directors of local police department, real estate bureau, or transportation agencies, these corrupt officials accumulate bribes in millions.

---

68   Data collected by the author from the China General Social Survey (CGSS) 2015 database.

In Mr. Chen's defense, he was referring to entry-level public servants when he said "becoming an official." Most entry-level public servants like himself have no opportunity even to accept bribes, let alone making millions. If one removes corruption from the picture, government officials even up to the senior politicians in Beijing do not earn nearly as much as company managers on the book. Whereas in the private sector salaries often increase substantially as one climbs up the ladder, compensations increase rather insignificantly within the *danwei* system. Even if Mr. Chen receives promotions to the level equivalent to a director of a local bureau, he likely will not see a substantial improvement in his financial conditions.

Many entry-level public servants in China are dissatisfied, but they are far from desperate. As Chapter 3 shows, most of them still earn more than an average urban citizen and they are in no way at risk of slipping into poverty. Though they are not financially free from worries, so are their peers in the private sector. At the same time, that dissatisfaction is in no way insignificant, especially for many young *danwei* employees who already face increasing financial pressures with an existing mortgage and imminent and long-term expenditure on childcare and education.

"I know comparing myself with my peers while having a nicely furnished apartment and a stable job sounds petty and shallow," Mr. Chen looked at me with an apologetic smile near his lips. "but it's not so when you have just enough to support yourself..."

Not knowing how to respond, I replied, "It must be really difficult."

Mr. Chen sighed and looked out the window. "What happens after I get married and have children? What happens if my parents fall sick? There are just too many ifs that each costs a fortune."

I stared out of the window at the adjacent building with him silently.

Realizing he went slightly off track, Mr. Chen turned around and said, "to get back to your question, I am happy with what I have, but at the same time, I am not so happy."

CHAPTER 7

STRUCTURE OF ENTRAPMENT

———

The moment I walk into any *danwei* building in Hefei, I feel an eerie sense of discomfort. It's not that anything stands out as particularly unusual or different. If anything, it's that absolutely *nothing* stands out as unusual or different. In almost every *danwei,* building I see the same *faux* marble stairs and pristine white walls, the same black-and-white tiles and furniture, and the same slogans or banners. I would not go as far as to say an air of repression hangs above me, but I certainly feel an intangible weight stifling my creative and adventurous urge. The strong sense of confinement and control has lingered in the marble halls of danwei buildings since the 1950s. Welcome to the flip side of public servants' economic security.

Though my observation and sentiment may seem exaggerated, many *danwei* employees I interviewed expressed similar feelings, often complaining about the *danwei* career and the surrounding environment as "rigid," "unexciting," or "monotonous." For most of the entry-level public servants I interviewed, daily assignments consist mostly of repetitive and often trivial tasks requiring no particular skill. Their dull, repetitive assignments remind me of what Weber terms the "iron cage." Criticizing the increased rationalization driven by teleological efficiency, calculation, and control, Weber coined this term to describe a new sense of entrapment and disenchantment.

Visualize Weber's iron cage as McDonald's, the famous fast-food chain. Opened by the McDonald brothers in 1840, McDonald's (then named McDonald's Bar-B-Que) started as a drive-in restaurant in California. In 1848, the brothers made the risky decision to streamline their operations by offering only a limited menu and redesigned the kitchen to maximize efficiency. After joining the company in 1954, Ray Kroc helped expand McDonald's to a truly global fast food restaurant chain. While having over 38,000 locations worldwide, McDonald's has preserved its essence. The menus, despite regional variations, remain limited. All food items are prepared in the same way according to a set recipe. So a Big Mac is a Big Mac whether you order it in the US or across the world in China.

In 1993, Sociologist George Ritzer coined the term "McDonaldization" to describe the rationalization of production, work, and consumption that became prominent in the late twentieth century. Observing the unique management practices hailed by the successful fast-food chain, Ritzer theorized four elements of McDonaldization—efficiency, calculability, predictability, and control.[69] The end result of McDonaldization is a standardized product or service performed with the minimal time and resources required, which affects both the production and consumer experience.

McDonaldization is "an amplification and extension of Weber's theory of rationalization," which for Weber was the cornerstone of bureaucracy.[70] It embodies contemporary rationalization, or the search for the optimum means to a specific end, which produces a series of rules, regulations, and social structures highlighting efficiency and control.

Despite its obvious advantages, McDonaldization suffers from what Ritzer terms as "irrationality of rationality." Production, service, and consumer experiences at McDonald's are highly dehumanized as the pursuit for efficiency and predictability reduces the enchantment of risk and uncertainty. The introduction of self-serving kiosks and contact-free services only further minimizes the already trained and uniform interactions between service providers and customers at McDonald's, further alienating all participants from their work, service, and experience.

The marked similarity between China's *danwei* system and Weber's bureaucracy does not come as a surprise because the *danwei* system, by design, is an effective bureaucratic structure. Such similarity is also ironic if one considers the former a communist and socialist institution. Around the same time Weber analyzed bureaucracy as a paradigm of rationality,

---

69   George Ritzer, *The McDonaldization of Society*, 20th Anniversary ed, (London: Sage Publications, 2013), 13-15.

70   Ibid., 29.

Marx offered fierce criticism against the oppression of the working class by the capitalist pursuit of efficiency that led to the alienation of labor. As a Marxist structure of production and governance, China's *danwei* system has failed to liberate its employees from the iron cage of alienation.

This paradoxical nature of *danwei* derives from its socialist origin in the 1950s. As a counterpart of the rural commune system, the urban *danwei* structure played the intermediary role between the state and the individuals.[71] During a time when China was secluded from much of the Western world and the image of this oriental mystery resembled much like what North Korea looks like to foreigners today, the central government had direct control over the entire social and economic landscape. In urban areas, this meant all formal employees—be they public servants, schoolteachers, or factory workers—belonged to their respective work units. For the state, work units served as a tool for governance, control, and mobilization efficiently and effectively; for the individuals, their respective *danwei* functioned as a place of employment, residence, and social interactions.

As mentioned in Chapter 2, the pre-reform *danwei* resembled a "total institution" that broke down the ordinary barrier between sleep, work, and play. Within walled and gated compounds, work units offered secured lifetime employment and all-encompassing social welfare including housing allocation, healthcare provision, education for children, cafeteria, barbershop, and public bath. In return, every aspect of daily life,

---

71 Chun Zhang and Yanwei Chai, "Un-gated and Integrated Work Unit Communities in Post-Socialist Urban China: A Case Study from Beijing," *Habitant International* 43 (March 2014): 87.

from work and school to leisure activities and private matters, all happened within the *danwei* compound.

From the perspective of spatial governance, the *danwei* structure achieved remarkable success. The intermediary role *danwei* played enabled efficient mass mobilization for central campaigns. The enclosed nature of walled compounds also effectively regulated social movements without much negative repercussion. In the US, gated residential communities fostered and reinforced class consciousness by "keeping the outsiders out;" China's pre-reform *danwei* compounds served the role of "keeping in insiders in." But most *danwei* employees didn't view their circumstances as rigidity or entrapment. Having witnessed years of war, famine, and disaster, many found security, protection, and identity within *danwei*'s walls.

China's urban landscape underwent a dramatic transformation in the 1980s. By the late 1990s and early 2000s, China formally abolished the housing allocation system, discontinuing the decades-long practice of welfare housing.[72] Compared to the pre-reform *danwei* compounds, the newly constructed residential quarters, though they remain gated and often manned by security guards, are highly limited in scope, influence, and control.

No longer confined behind gates and walls, many young *danwei* employees in the 1990s embraced this newfound freedom, challenging the unconditional loyalty toward their work

---

72　Li Hanlin and Li Lulu,中国的单位组织: 资源、权力与交换 (*China's Danwei System: Resource, Power, and Exchange*) (Beijing: Life Bookstore Publishing, 2019), 4-7; Li Lulu, "论 '单位' 研究 (Danwei Study)," *Sociological Studies* 17 no. 5 (May 2002): 23-32.

units and actively criticizing the institution for its rigidity and tendency to corruption. Despite their appreciation for freedom and independence from the total institution that governed and dictated the lives of their parents, most of them, now senior employees in *danwei* in terms of age, maintain close links with their work units—living in *danwei* allocated or sponsored housing units built in the early 2000s, dining at work unit cafeterias, and spending leisure time with colleagues. Many senior public servants I interviewed considered themselves more independent than previous generations, but when asked about their daily routines and social interactions, many of their answers revealed strong influences exerted by their *danwei*. While their work units no longer tear down the barriers between their work, sleep, and leisure, most *danwei* employees still share the same circles with their colleagues as they work in the same building and live in the same community. In other words, the previously small, enclosed compound has transformed into a large, porous, and invisible dome.

Earlier generations of public servants in China viewed gated compounds and the invisible dome as protection rather than entrapment. Younger employees, Mr. Chen says, feel "chained by a pair of shackles around their ankles." Despite the craze for a *danwei* career among contemporary youth in China, the whole concept of a work unit is full of unresolved contradictions. Every rationale for joining a *danwei* only sows the seed for a reason to reject it. For millions of young people growing up with a booming economy and relatively open society, their dream for a society that allows the manifestation of their individualities is shattered by the reality that encourages obedient clones.

Danwei's iron rice bowl is a double-edged sword of security and entrapment. Secure lifetime employment and the monotonic environment slowly drain away employees' enthusiasm and creativity; *Danwei*'s political control through ideology and the predictable path of promotion further restrict individualism and deters thinking outside the box.[73]

During my interviews, almost everyone mentioned the need to "obey the orders from the superior" or "making the superior happy" in order to survive comfortably and land promotions. Mr. Li, who holds a more optimistic view than Mr. Chen, calls the *danwei* environment rigid but not completely restraining.

"Good ideas still emerge and policy innovations can still happen," Mr. Li said, but ultimately, it all depends on whether "you can please your superior."

"And what's the best way to do that?" I probed.

"While in most cases the smartest choice is to remain silent and maybe save your brilliant but unwelcoming ideas for later," Mr. Li paused and sipped at his tea. "But if you are really clever," he smiled, "then the best practice is to convince your superior that your new, innovative idea is in fact his own creation and you are just a source of inspiration."

---

73   Victor N. Shaw, *Social Control in China: A Study of Chinese Work Units* (Westport: Praeger Publishers, 1996), 31-33.

One is allowed to think outside the box in the work unit system if he or she can move the box around to make the idea inside the box.

Besides the inherent rigidity of the *danwei* system, indifference toward technical skills further reinforces this sense of entrapment for young public servants. Most *danwei* employees hold bachelor's or master's degrees in specific, often technical fields such as engineering and communication. Experts on China have pointed out the proliferation of technocrats in China. From Xi Jinping who studied chemical engineering to Mr. Chen who majored in electronic communication in college, many government decision makers and employees share similar backgrounds in their technical skills.

When Mr. Chen joined public service after graduation, he hoped to make unique contributions with his background in communication. He soon discovered that "everyone inside the *danwei* system has but one major: public administration (行政)," which translates to "serving the superior" in Mr. Chen's blunt explanation. Even social sciences students see few opportunities to apply their professional knowledge to daily tasks. Mr. Dong, a history major, also complained about the discrepancy between his university education and the limited and trivial skills required for a *danwei* job.

Among retired and current *danwei* employees, the younger generation stands out as the most conscious and critical of the rigidity of the *danwei* system. When compared to many young college graduates in the 1990s who left their work units for risky opportunities, however, contemporary youth appear much less adventurous and courageous. Some senior public servants I interviewed complained about the lack of aspiration and determination among contemporary youth. Such a view oversimplifies the current situation. Today's young people may appear more complacent, more calculated, and more risk averse, but most of them do not agree with such characterizations. The fact that millions of young people are willing to accept and even compete for a "pair of shackles" may suggest that the society, rather than the young people themselves, are to blame for the structure of entrapment that clearly and painfully dominates the life of Chinese youth.

PART FOUR

HER CHINESE DREAM

把男女平等作为促进我国社会
发展的一项基本国策

江泽民　1995年9月4日于第四次世界妇女大会

*We will make gender equality one of our basic
national policies to promote social development.*

JIANG ZEMIN AT THE FOURTH WORLD CONFERENCE
ON WOMEN ON SEPTEMBER 4, 1995

CHAPTER 8

WOMEN AND SOCIALIST EGALITARIANISM

———

For members of China's youth generation, myself included, foot binding seems a castigated practice from a distant past. The once glorified beauty and eroticism of bowed, pointed, and deformed feet of merely three inches long and half an inch wide had disappeared from Chinese society. Physical appearance is still glorified and sexualized, but cultural fetishization of feet—any feet—seems absurd. The practice represents a shameful, backward part of China's imperial history. This once popular and upper-class custom, however, is not so far removed as we may think.

My understanding of foot binding was informed not by history books but by my own family's history. It was the year I ended primary school. My great grandmother just died, a traumatic experience for a six-year-old.

I have only vague, episodic memories about my great grandmother, and often I cannot even distinguish whether a certain recollection is my own recollection or construction from photos and videos. In my most vivid memory of her, she was resting peacefully in a dim room. My mother stood next to me in a room full of relatives. I do not remember whether I cried that day, but when I looked down at my great grandmother's body lying in the glass coffin, I wondered whether she would wake up and walk toward me at any moment.

Strangely, I cannot picture her walking. Whenever I visited her, I seldom saw her walking around the house. Until recently, I had never given it a second thought: after all, my great grandmother was already ninety when I was born and she enjoyed spending her days sunbathing on the balcony. Everything changed when I came across Gerry Mackie's paper on foot binding and infibulation—"Ending Footbinding and Infibulation: A Convention Account"—while researching for a sociology paper. I never saw my great grandmother walking because her feet were bound.[74] I recalled my mother's fleeting comment once on how great grandmother's feet were tiny. I had known about foot binding practices for over a decade, but I never connected the dots. The sudden realization brought me a sense of unease as something once so remote and ridiculous became not only familiar but also extremely personal.

WOMEN HOLD UP HALF THE SKY

The dissonance between discarded traditions and modernity reflects the utter transformation of the Chinese society

---

74 Gerry Mackie, "Ending Footbinding and Infibulation: A Convention Account," *American Sociological Review* 61, no. 6 (December 1996): 999-1017.

during the twentieth century, an era defined by rapid political, social, and economic change. The foot binding practice
ended in a single generation. While social progress did not
occur instantaneously, the Communist revolution culminat-
ing with the establishment of the regime in Beijing in 1949
completely rewrote China's entire landscape at an unprecedented pace.

Atrocities committed by Mao Zedong have earned him the
reputation as an infamous dictator, but the women liberation campaign (妇女解放运动) has often been interpreted as
Mao's least disputed legacy. Gender equality first became one
of the main concerns for Chinese intellectuals in the New
Culture Movements in the 1910s and 1920s. After founding
the People's Republic on October 1, 1949, Mao prioritized
the rights of women in the Marxist-Communist context.[75]
Seven months later, Mao delivered the New Marriage Law,
promising equal rights for men and women.

The New Marriage Law radically changed the existing gender dynamics and rewrote how families are structured in
China. It established a new democratic marriage system that
promised freedom of marriage, outlawed polygamy, guaranteed gender equality, and abolished arranged marriages.[76]
Women were allowed to keep their last names and divorce
their husbands. Men were forbidden from divorcing their
wives during pregnancy. The statute also challenged the
traditional gender dynamics stipulated upon the gendered

---

75 Meng Ke, "毛泽东遗产争议：妇女能顶半边天 (Controversies over Mao's
    Legacy: Women Hold up Half of the Sky)," BBC, December 24, 2013.
76 "中华人民共和国婚姻法 (Marriage Law of the People's Republic of
    China)," *People's Daily*, April 16, 1950, 1.

division of labor and specified equal rights and responsibilities within each household.

The new Communist regime took steps to incorporate gender equality within the society as well. Guided by Mao's famous phrase—"women hold up half of the sky (妇女撑起半边天)"—the state encouraged and sometimes required women to actively participate in the workforce, though often driven by political considerations. In urban areas, the state organized both men and women through the *danwei* system that provided them with stable employment and various welfare (housing, education, and insurance). At the same time, the work unit system served as an organ for political control. The mass mobilization of men and women to participate in the labor force to construct a new, modernized society provided unprecedented education opportunities for women, significantly reducing the illiteracy rate in China.[77]

For many women who came from a rural background, this rapid social change was particularly liberating. For the first time, Chinese women were no longer expected to stay at home. They could enter the workforce without judgment from their family and society. Going to their workplaces opened doors for greater social participation among other women of similar backgrounds. And their new opportunities to work and earn salaries outside the home elevated the status of women within the household to an equal partner to their husbands.[78]

---

77   William Lavely et al, "The Rise in Female Education in China: National and Regional Patterns," *The China Quarterly* no. 121, 64-73.

78   Zuo Jiping, "20世纪50年代的妇女解放和男女义务平等: 中国城市夫妻的经历与感受 (Women's Liberation and Equality in Male-Female

Driven by the Marxist interpretation of gender dynamics and family structures, the Chinese Communist Party (CCP) sought to liberate women from the household slavery system. The party-state portrayed images of active female participation in political, social, and economic propaganda campaigns. The government then used these images to mobilize women, especially in the rural areas, to meet the increasing labor demand for economic development. A famous example of China's propaganda showcases the famous female tractor driver, Liang Jun—also known as the "tractor girl." Liang Jun rose to fame when the third series of Renminbi (RMB) featured her on the 1 RMB bill in 1962.[79] Since then, she has been a popular icon of female liberation and women's service to the construction of the great nation.

The Red Detachment of Women, a movie depicting a company of brave female soldiers during WWII, continued to popularize women as key contributors to revolutionary causes. The movie won public attention after winning the best picture, best director, and best actress for the first Hundred Flowers Awards (百花奖), one of the most prestigious film awards in China, in 1962. It also became an undying classic after the success of the *Red Detachment of Women* ballet in 1964. By the end of 1966, the script was elevated to one of eight "revolutionary model theatrical works (革命样板戏)."

A closer look at the propaganda work during the Mao era also reveals the ubiquitous presence of women from the depiction

Responsibilities in the 1950s: Experience of Urban Couples in China)," *Chinese Journal of Sociology* 25, no. 1 (2005): 182-209.

79 "Liang Jun: China's First Female Tractor Driver, and National Icon, Dies," BBC, January 15, 2020.

of the revolutionary mass. Though these female figures often represented occupations that conform to traditional gender roles of care services such as nurse and teacher, they were also frequently cast as farmers and sometimes revolutionary soldiers. In other words, the party-state recognized the indispensable role women had played within the society without proscribing them from activities and occupations traditionally considered within the realm of men.

The elevation of women's status for mass mobilization and economic development is not unique to China. WWII witnessed waves of female empowerment movements across developed countries as acute labor shortages drove millions of women into factories and shipyards, filling in the jobs once occupied by men who were sent off to war. To convince women, many of them mothers with husbands on the frontlines and children at home, to serve in the war effort, governments sought to inspire patriotism with posters enticing women to serve their countries. The most famous of these images, Rosie the Riveter, depicts a confident American woman wearing a red bandana and flexing her muscles under the headline, "We Can Do It!" Though designed as a call for patriotism, Rosie the Riveter also came to serve as a symbol and an inspiration for female liberation as it popularized a different way of portraying women. Similarly, the image of Liang Jun driving a tractor while wearing bandana aroused strong sentiments in China, inspiring many young women to dedicate themselves to serve the nation. The parallel between Rosie the Riveter and Liang Jun the tractor girl reveals similarities in how state-sponsored mobilization campaigns help elevate women's social status. It does not, however, preclude striking differences between the Chinese "women's liberation" campaign and the women's empowerment movement in the US.

Compared to the US mobilization effort that responded to the exigent crisis, the Chinese campaign was more profound and systematic. The mobilization of US women during WWII led to long-term changes in gender dynamics, but mass employment for women proved only a temporary measure. As soon as the war ended, American women were encouraged to return home and become model housewives. The Chinese party-state, on the other hand, envisioned long-term mass mobilization of both men and women for constructing a socialist China. The CCP cast itself as a revolutionary force seeking to completely break away from the obsolete, corrupted feudalism that had doomed the Chinese people at the hands of Western imperialist power. Rejecting the Confucian moral code of three obediences and four virtues (三从四德) naturally became an important campaign for the young state. The three obediences stipulate women to obey their fathers as maiden daughters, their husbands as wives, and their sons as widows. The four virtues, on the other hand, requires feminine virtue in ethics (妇德), speech (妇言), manner and appearance (妇容), and works (妇功). What replaced these traditional gender dynamics that long dominated Chinese society was a classless society of gender equality.

Many institutions that defined the Socialist era in China—from the rural collectivities to the urban *danwei*—incorporated the Marxist ideals of egalitarianism. Within the *danwei* system, for example, all employees, regardless of gender, worked and lived within the same enclosed compounds, enjoyed the same welfare and benefits, and received equal pay for equal rank. No longer bound completely to domestic chores and their husbands' orders, Chinese women enjoyed greater independence and autonomy from the burden of the family that had restrained their social roles and status for millennia.[80]

WOMANHOOD IN SERVICE TO THE STATE

The women's liberation campaign, however, did not create a rosy utopia of gender equality. While the iconoclast spirits rejected ancient patriarchal practices, the new Communist regime demanded complete loyalty from its citizens. While the state waved the banner of gender equality, the hierarchical political structure that had a firm grasp on the lives of individual Chinese citizens was predominantly, if not exclusively, controlled by men. Thus many inveterate values and beliefs that once justified and sustained the now jettisoned practices remained.

Increasing women's participation in the work force to share the burden of supporting the family, however, did not encourage greater male participation in domestic chores. In this sense, the new gender dynamics were constructed upon a dual standard. Outside the family, husbands and wives were comrades sharing equal responsibilities, but within each household, the gendered division of labor persisted.[81] As women broke the traditional boundary and stepped into a world previously dominated by men, the opposite boundary remained. The state needed more manpower for developing

---

80 Zuo, "Women's Liberation and Equality," 182-209.
81 Ibid.

socialism and found that in women. But it was always about the state's needs, not the elevation of women's standing. In fact, during the campaign for women's liberation and mass mobilization, individual wills were oppressed and family interests were grossly overlooked. In the name of serving the country, many women reduced their commitments to family and children, abandoned all their free time, and sacrificed their health.[82]

More importantly, the principle of gender equality advocated by the CCP hardly reflects the actual conditions of gender dynamics within China during the Mao era. In reality women's liberation during the 1950s and 1960s was marked by repression of female identity rather than a celebration of femininity. In the same posters that glorified and praised women's contribution to the construction of the socialist nation, women's sexuality was barely evident. Body curves were missing, though scant attention was paid to the breast in some posters in order to distinguish a woman from a man. Motherhood was never represented by pregnant women even in posters advocating for family planning.

During the Cultural Revolution, the state even encouraged women to conform to the "neutralization in gender."[83] Women wore drab uniforms, cut their hair short, and zealously dedicated their lives to revolutionary activities, pillaging cultural relics, and publicly denouncing and humiliating (批斗) intellectuals and counterrevolutionaries. The image

---

82 Ibid.

83 Hong Quan, "The Representation and/or Repression of Chinese Women: From A Socialist Aesthetics to Commodity Fetish," *Neohelicon* 46 (2019): 728.

of the red guard (红卫兵), or para-military students swearing loyalty to Mao, completely denounced and rejected all feminine elements and desexualized the female gender. To become a red guard, many women cleared their wardrobes of gowns, dresses, and high heels. They threw away cosmetics and adopted new habits and patterns of speech, denouncing feminine elegance while embracing masculine fortitude and boorishness.[84]

Through the discourse of revolution and the slogan of serving the country, the state replaced the family and gained complete control of women, including reproduction, marriage, education, and employment.[85] The traditional morality of women's obedience to their fathers, husbands, and sons had been replaced by the revolutionary notion of obedience to the state and to the *danwei* in the urban context. In this sense, Chinese women were never liberated during the Socialist era. Subjectively, many felt liberation from imperialist oppression, impoverishment, and absolute obedience to their husbands. Such mentality, however, reflects the unfortunate truth that the women's liberation movement prioritized loyalty to the state while ignoring individual rights.[86] Furthermore, the state repressed women's subjectivity in the promotion of desexualized gender neutrality, reducing their identities to a collective being without individual consciousness.[87]

---

84 Zhou Xiaoli, "中国女性的身体与革命性 (The Body and Revolutionary Spirit of Chinese Women)," Intellectuals, published March 30, 2018.

85 Quan, "The Representation and/or Repression," 728.

86 Zuo, "Women's Liberation and Equality," 182-209.

87 Quan, "The Representation and/or Repression," 727.

The Opening and Reform campaign launched in the late 1970s spelled an end to the tumultuous socialist period under Mao's leadership. The women's liberation campaign and the systematic desexualization of Chinese women, however, had lasting impacts on Chinese society. Women's expanding role in the workforce contributed to an elevation of their status. This change is most evident within the *danwei* system, a rare relic echoing the Socialist era. Contemporary *danwei* maintains the principle of egalitarianism by promising equal pay for equal rank, regardless of age, gender, and performance. The permanent employment, or iron rice bowl, of a *danwei* position also precludes gender discrimination in firing or demotion and guarantees a secure and stable career path for women. This, in turn, offers female *danwei* employees a level of financial independence that is essential to female empowerment.

When economic reforms abolished the planned economic systems and paved the way for the influx of foreign goods and ideas, practices and norms of female desexualization ended. The transition away from decades of repression was sudden and turbulent. Young women embraced the new freedom brought by the market economy, mechanisms repressing female subjectivity weakened or disappeared, and a new wave of feminine re-sexualization swept across China. This rebirth of femininity was met with the commodification and objectification of women, a trend that continued to shape contemporary gender dynamics and impact Chinese women's pursuit of prosperity and equality.

CHAPTER 9

WOMEN AND CAPITALISM

One of the biggest cultural shocks I learned in the United States, believe it or not, was that Kentucky Fried Chicken (KFC) was not actually "fancy." Unlike in China, where KFC restaurants occupy prime locations in city centers and offer an array of delicacies ranging from beef steak wraps to vegetable egg drop soups, the more "authentic" American KFCs are more often found in remote locations with much more limited menu options. Suffice to say, I was "a bit" disappointed.

Growing up, a trip to the Chinese KFC was my dream. My parents offered it as a reward if I received good grades at school, while hosting a birthday party and treating my friends with "the pinnacle of western cuisine" there earned total bragging rights.

Eight years after China and the US established formal diplomatic relations, KFC opened its first restaurant in Beijing.

The large, three-story establishment located at the center of the capital housed more than five-hundred seats, breaking the world record of the largest fast-food restaurant. It was 1987, and the promise of tasting Western cuisine with around 5 RMB ($1.3) attracted thousands of Chinese to visit this novel establishment and take part in the new trend of embracing everything Western. On the first day of opening, the Beijing KFC earned more than 300,000 RMB—equally selling over forty-thousand combo meals. Though no longer a rare sight in China, fast food restaurants such as KFC and McDonald's still embody Western culture in China. Their success and immediate popularity in China in the 1980s and 1990s attested to the rapid change in the Chinese society brought by the introduction of capitalism and Western ideas.

NEW FREEDOM, NEW WOMANHOOD

For millions of Chinese, the era of economic reform was not only a time of greater economic privatization and financial autonomy but also a new age of unprecedented freedom. As China established or strengthened diplomatic and commercial ties with former capitalist enemies and invited foreign companies to invest in the Chinese labor and consumer markets, Western culture and ideas also gained a new group of followers and admirers. Inspired by the new liberal atmosphere that encourages individuality and adventurism instead of the Socialist collectivist ideals, talented artists spearheaded a new movement in Chinese aesthetics that challenged the drab Socialist landscape of lifeless grey. Influx of foreign goods and cultures also fundamentally changed how Chinese understand themselves and the world around them.

For Chinese women, the new reform era brought with it a completely different reality—one paradoxically defined both by an unprecedented degree of liberation yet new restrictions, inequality, and stratifications. The rejection of the Socialist "gender neutrality" liberated Chinese women from the imposed restrictions on their femininity and subjectivity. But the re-sexualization of the Chinese women did not overthrow the inveterate patriarchy within the society. Instead of gaining a fully independent voice of their own, they fell victim to the commodification of the female body. Thus for almost half of China's population, the success story of China's economic miracle is at best a two-sided coin, one of opportunity and prosperity, and the other of inequality and even injustice.

A key theme to the reform era is liberation of the self from the collectivities such as enclosed *danwei* compounds physically surrounded by iron gates and concrete walls. For many women, it also means regaining their voices and identity as women, rather than a "gender-neutral" subject of the state. Doffing the drab, monochromatic jackets of green and blue, Chinese women rediscovered traditional aesthetics embodied in *qipao* (mandarin gown) or embraced Western styles of clothing that constituted the new modernity. Makeup, once denounced during the Socialist era as capitalist and thus counterrevolutionary, found its way back to the dressing tables in China. *Danwei* employees were no exceptions. Even though the hallways, offices, and furniture look almost identical across different government buildings—the uniform black and white tiles, matching wooden table and white file cabinets, and the same aloof, insipid ambiance—uniformity no longer defines China's public employees.

Danwei hallway. Photo by the author.

Contemporary public employees are avid contributors to China's rapidly expanding market for beauty products, driven by young and low-tier city consumers. During my visits to various *danwei* buildings, I caught not a faint whiff of the remnants of the era of desexualization, especially from the younger generations. They are economically secured, financially independent, and confident about their own femininity. Compared to their parents and grandparents, they demonstrated no fear, shame, or reluctance embracing who they are as women and celebrating their beauty and individualities.

MARKETIZATION OF FEMALE SEXUALITY

The story of economic reform was not completely a tale of liberation for Chinese women. The retreat of the state in economic activities invited new forms of gender discrimination and stratification. In recent years, less women are participating in the labor force and the gender pay gap has widened. A 2013 research concluded women in China are paid 75 percent of the wages of their male counterparts.[88] While this number has increased since according to some sources, in 2018 the gender pay gap still stood over 20 percent.[89] A 2018 report by the World Economic Forum ranked China's gender parity in 103th place out of 149 countries, a tenth consecutive fall from its 57th rank in 2008.[90] Under the pretext of avoiding unnecessary expenditures such as paid maternity leaves and stereotypical assumptions that men are more fit for jobs requiring frequent business trips, companies favored men over women during their hiring process. Public recruiting advertisements frequently included gender in the

---

88 Lin Xiu and Morley Gunderson, "Gender Earnings Differences in China: Base Pay, Performance Pay, and Total Pay," *Contemporary Economic Policy* 31, no. 1 (2013): 235-254.

89 Zheng Yangpeng, "Chinese Women Earn A Fifth Less Than Men and The Gap Is Widening Fast, Survey by Online Recruiter Boss Zhipin Finds," *South China Morning Post*, March 7, 2019.

90 World Economic Forum, *The Global Gender Gap Report 2018* (Geneva: World Economic Forum, 2018), 11.

requirements. From low-paying jobs such as security guards to high-paying, prestigious positions in technology companies such as Baidu, women were not even offered a chance to compete for a position with their male counterparts.[91] In 2016, Baidu's filming program published an ad stating the requirements for a manager: "strong logical reasoning ability, effective execution skills...graceful men and manly women."[92] The slang term "manly women (女汉子)" refers to women with masculine traits, such as being less sensitive and independent. These "men only" and "men preferred" job advertisements reflect the discriminatory view that women are physically, intellectually, and psychologically less capable than men.

Insular from the cost-reduction ethos and market-driven mentalities prevalent in the private sector, the *danwei* society upholds a very different gender dynamic within the workplace. Influenced by the socialist egalitarian values, work units determine their employees' salaries based on their rank and regardless of their age or gender. The lifetime employment system guarantees no demotion or firing in the event of pregnancy or childcare. In fact, *danwei* employees enjoy a much longer maternal leave than their counterparts in the private sector. Compared to the ninety-eight-day maternity leave granted by most private companies in accordance with the law, many female *danwei* employees, including Ms. Zhang, can take a period of leave for up to 150 days. When she returned from her leave of absence, Ms. Zhang simply

---

91 Human Rights Watch, *"Only Men Need Apply": Gender Discrimination in Job Advertisements in China* (New York: Human Rights Watch, 2018), 2.

92 Ibid., 17, 18.

picked up where she left off five months ago without any worry that someone else replaced her while away.

Another major difference between the private and public sector, according to Ms. Zhang, is the recruiting process. Compared to the unpredictable procedure in private companies in which success or failure often depends on the whim and subjective judgement of recruiters, the application process for a public service career constitutes a standardized exam and an interview process for the top few applicants. The standardized exam, which differs in questions between the national and provincial levels and between each province, consists of two segments: the administrative aptitude test (行政职业能力测试 or 行测 for short) and free response essay (申论). The first comprises over 130 questions to be answered in two hours on five topics: common sense (常识), language comprehension (语言理解), quantitative knowledge (数量关系), logic and deduction (判断推理), and information analysis (资料分析).[93] The free response essay segment, on the other hand, consists of several short- to medium-length prompts asking the test takers to synthesize, interpret, and offer opinions and policy recommendations on provided reading materials. Trained throughout their adolescent years to excel in standardized tests, Chinese youth find more comfort and predictability in the *danwei* path, and for women especially, it means less discrimination and greater empowerment. In fact, Ms. Zhang's work unit has hired much more women than men in recent years because most top contestants that pass the standardized tests are women in the first place.

---

93   For sample questions of administrative aptitude test, see Appendix.

For many women fighting for security and promotion inside private companies while juggling work and family, the *danwei* path seems like a utopia free of discrimination and unspoken rules against women. Indeed, many women I interviewed, including Ms. Zhang, admitted their fortune working as a public servant. "I am free to choose the right balance for my life. When I want to spend more time taking care of my family, no one will punish me for leaving work early, and whenever I am ready to devote myself 100 percent back to work again, my position is always reserved for me."

The *danwei* environment is not completely immune from the changes brought by rapid marketization. The reclamation of femininity did free Chinese women from the control of the state but not the patriarchal order that has long dominated the Chinese society. Though beauty is no longer scorned upon with disdain, women had little power in deciding what constitutes the standard of beauty. Since the early days of reform era, mass media has played an indispensable role in formulating the conception of body image and feminine beauty. As Caucasian models dominated advertisements in magazines and billboards for products ranging from cosmetics and feminine products to clothing items, Chinese mass media communicated new, Western standards of ideal beauty. Driven by the urge to reclaim femininity, Chinese women pursued this thin-idealized beauty that puts heavy emphasis on slim body shape.

In recent years, China has evolved to become a major market for Korean fashion trends due to the influx of Korean television dramas, pop music, and entertainment. The Korean Wave also brought new standards of beauty. Similar to traditional Chinese aesthetics, the contemporary Korean image of beauty emphasizes pale skin, big eyes, high nose bridges, and pointy jaws. Driven by these new, often unnatural standards of beauty, China's cosmetic and plastic surgery markets took off as millions of young girls invested in beauty products to bring themselves closer to the idealized version.

Many of the Chinese women who conform to these idealized standards do so for external reasons. Femininity has become commercialized and commodified in the patriarchal market economy. Companies use attractive women to attract qualified male applicants, female models are frequently objectified as sexy symbols to cater to male customers, and hiring ads often include strict requirements for women such as height, age, and etiquette.[94]

Objectification of feminine beauty changes the gender dynamics in Chinese workplace, replacing the socialist egalitarianism with a discriminatory structure that treats men and women differently. In her studies on China's service industry, Amy Hanser introduced the concept of the "rice bowl of youth," highlighting the practice of favoring young, pretty female employees and associating the sexualized feminine identity with capitalist modernity.[95] In fact, the "rice bowl of youth" is not unique to the service industry, which seeks to promote distinction that caters to a specific group of customers, especially those well-endowed with economic and cultural capital. Even in the enclosed *danwei*

---

94 Human Rights Watch, *Only Men Need Apply*, 31-36.

95 Amy Hanser, *Service Encounter: Class, Gender, and the Market for Social Distinction in Urban China* (Stanford: Stanford University Press, 2008), 17-18, 97-99.

environment, youth and beauty often become assets for young female employees.

Mrs. Chen recounted me her personal experience with the "rice bowl of youth." Back in the early 2000s, the director of Mrs. Chen's *danwei* needed a temporary secretary and typist for a provincial level summit. Well known within the work unit as the prettiest employee and a fast typist, Mrs. Chen was handpicked by the director for the temporary position. While the honor to serve as the director's personal attaché during a high-level meeting did not her bring any tangible benefits such a raise or a promotion, Mrs. Chen became a star in the office, the one chosen by the director. Interestingly, Mrs. Chen demonstrated no sign of dissatisfaction regarding how her beauty was objectified or how she was selected not primarily because of her skill but rather because of her looks. Although few female public servants I interviewed shared similar experience with Mrs. Chen, almost all confirmed the ubiquitous practice of the "rice bowl of youth," especially in service work.

From the points of view of most female public servants I interviewed, the economic reform has liberated Chinese women from the tight grip of the state and opened new opportunities for them to define their identities. At the same time, however, marketization has undone many legacies of the "women liberation" campaign. Though laws guaranteeing equal rights for men and women remain in effect, they fail to translate into equal opportunity and protection inside the workplace or family. Companies blatantly set gender preferences in their hiring ads, discouraging women from skilled, high-paying positions. Since economic liberalization, women's participation in the work force has been on a steady decline and the gender pay gap has widened. Amidst sweeping changes from China's economic reform, the *danwei* system stands as one of the last few remnants of the Socialist era upholding egalitarian values of gender equality in the workplace. To this end, the public sector has resisted many structural changes to gender dynamics found in the private sector driven by the supposed goal of cost reduction and the belief that a female employee must expend much of her time and energy on family and childcare. The *danwei* system seems conducive to gender equality.

Even so, the *danwei* environment is not completely shielded from mounting gender inequalities that defined the reform era. The re-sexualization of the feminine identity transformed women from gender-neutral subjects of the state— dutiful farmers, workers, soldiers, and mothers—to highly sexualized and commodified symbols of modernity. The ubiquity of the "rice bowl of youth," even within the *danwei* environment, reveals systemic roots of China's gender inequality. Youth and beauty might give a temporary edge, but they do not last. Within the persisting and rigid patriarchy, women are only winning the competition against older women but not their male colleagues. They would soon become disadvantaged by the very traits that once got them ahead. Thus is the story of entrenched gender inequality within Chinese society that neither the Socialist revolution nor the market reform has adequately addressed.

CHAPTER 10

WOMEN UNDER TRADITIONAL VALUES

———

"What kind of man would be a good match for you?" asked the dating counselor.

Qiu Huamei, a thirty-four-year-old lawyer, was searching for love. "I have high standards. For example, he must be well educated. More importantly, he must respect women. I mean, he should share housework with me."

"Sorry if I'm being too straightforward, but you're not beautiful in the traditional sense. I don't mean you're not pretty, I mean you're not a beauty. And also, you're old…"

"I'm old?"

"Yes, right?"

Ms. Qiu did not give in. "But I think I'm at a good age."

"Oh? Okay? Do you think you're at the perfect age for the marriage market? Please don't think you're in a good position. You might think you look young, but you're fooling yourself. Even if you fall in love with someone today, it would take at least a year to get married, one more to give birth, you'll be an old mom. This is the fastest track, right?"

"So what I meant earlier by respecting women is that what if I choose not to have children?"

The dating counselor could not believe what she just heard. "You have thoughts about not having children?"

"Why not?"

"I meant you want to find a man who can accept not having children?"

"Yes. So, so that's why I think…That's why I said I need someone who can respect my wishes."

"But do you want to be single or married right now?"

"Married, of course."

"Then you can't choose not to have children…It may be because of your job, but you have a tough personality…you will have to soften yourself up."

When Ms. Qiu walked into a dating counseling office, she was told bluntly that she was too old, not beautiful enough, and too tough. The excerpt from a documentary titled

Leftover Women revealed the challenges thousands of independent, well-educated women face in China today.[96] Under the pressure from family, friends, and the state, they seek a marriage that still allows them to stay true to their values, careers, and ambitions, but too often, they are pulled back by the invisible hand of traditional values that dictate what is right and wrong for a woman.

CULTURE, TRADITION AND PATRIARCHY

The twentieth century marked an era of transformation for Chinese society as new ideas confronted ancient traditions. Leaders and luminaries during this era sought to save China from shame at the hands of foreign powers by rejecting the traditional, dynastic values and mentalities that had long dominated the Chinese society. Republican leaders repelled the murk of superstitions and ignorance with Western concepts such as science and democracy. Communist revolutionaries went further, destroying all traces of feudalism, from ancient wisdom and traditional practices to even cultural relics.

Values, beliefs, and mentalities proved much more inveterate than practices and customs. This is particularly evident in China's gender dynamics. Though legally men and women have equal rights and duties, many traditional understandings of gender-specific roles and gendered division of labor remained. The most enduring perception that still impacts millions of women in China is the notion of separated

---

96 Leftover Women, directed by Shosh Shlam and Hilla Medalia (Boston: PBS, 2019), aired on PBS.

spheres, or "男主外,女主内" in Chinese, that men belong in the public sphere and women in the domestic.

Even during the height of culture revolution period when women actively participated in the work force, they still shouldered most responsibilities in the private sphere— rearing children, taking care of elderlies, and performing household chores. Though most women no longer depended on their husbands economically, few challenged this highly unequal arrangement. While championing egalitarianism, the state reinforced this notion of separated spheres. It glorified women's role as mothers but did not emphasize men's responsibility as fathers.

Such attitude became more apparent when official rhetoric later shifted from encouraging families to have more children to implementing the compulsory one-child policy to curb the high birth rate.

The disastrous famine wiped away millions of Chinese in the late 1950s and early 1960s. The baby boom that followed raised China's natural population growth rate to 27.5 per mille. The central government implemented family planning policies to restrain the sudden rise in birth rate. Under the slogan of "Insert intrauterine device (IUD) after one child, sterilize after two (一个上环, 两个绝育)," the Chinese government coerced countless women to have an IUD inserted or go through tubectomy. Men, the other piece of the puzzle, however, were largely left out of the picture. In 1983, China performed 17.7 million IUD insertions, 16.4 million tubecto-mies, 14.4 million abortions, and 4.26 million vasectomies.[97]

Figure 2. Birth control surgeries administered in China between 1971 and 2012. Data collected by the author from China's National Health Commission.

Under the banner of "women's liberation," the government promised to free Chinese women from the chains of feudalism and capitalism. In reality, the Chinese government has only reinforced the traditional concept that childcare—and to a large extent, the domestic sphere—falls under the responsibility of women, rather than jointly between husbands and wives. As the state demanded mass mobilization for building socialism, men were asked to place their duties toward the country before their identities as husbands and fathers. Throughout the implementation of the one-child

97 National Health and Family Planning Commission, 2013中国卫生统计年鉴 (China Health Statistics Yearbook 2013) (Beijing: National Health and Family Planning Commission, 2013), 242.

policy, vasectomy only accounted for at most 1 percent of all birth control surgeries administered.[98]

The gradual retreat of the state in the private sphere did not ameliorate gender inequality within the family. Private companies have actually reinforced the perception of separated spheres, often blatantly discriminating against female employees or applicants under the pretext of profit maximization. They view women as less qualified and less suitable for more skilled positions or more physically demanding jobs. Companies also frequently reject young female applicants believing they have less to offer to the company because women must devote their attention to childcare and the private sphere. Though companies seldom announce this belief and overtly use it to turn down potential candidates, many clearly prefer men or women with children in their hiring ads. The preference for married women with children stems from the desire to hire women no longer expected to take maternity leave, hence avoiding cost and loss of working time incurred when female employees take maternity leave.[99]

Compared to the global average, less women in China leave the workforce to become full-time mothers after pregnancy. Companies nevertheless seek to minimize the inconvenience and cost when making hiring decisions. Government regulations entitle women to at least ninety-eight days of paid maternity leave in China, so when a company welcomes a young, female employee, it must be prepared to "lose" three

---

98 Ibid.
99 Human Rights Watch, *"Only Men Need Apply": Gender Discrimination in Job Advertisements in China* (New York: Human Rights Watch, 2018), 28-29.

months to maternity leave. Few companies express concern over the potential cost of a male employee or applicant who will soon become a father. With no national stipulation on paternity leave, some provinces entitle men a maximum of thirty days' leave. Others guarantee none. Companies thus do not expect male employees to take too many days off after becoming a father.

On a daily basis, women also spend much more time on unpaid work than their husbands. On average, women spend fifty-three minutes a day on childcare whereas their male counterparts spend only seventeen minutes.[100] Among citizens between twenty-five to thirty-four, who spend the most time among all other age grounds on childcare, the gap becomes even more conspicuous. Women within that group spend 105 minutes per day; their husbands allocate barely twenty-nine.[101]

Domestic gender inequality does not end with childcare. Though more independent and better educated than they have ever been, Chinese women continue to shoulder the lion's share of housework. Men help out around the house for about forty-five minutes per day, while household responsibilities drain a whopping 126 minutes out of their wives' day.[102]

The perception of separated spheres and gendered division of labor is only the tip of the iceberg of gender inequality in

100 "2018年全国时间利用调查公报 (Report on National Time Usage in 2018)," National Bureau of Statistics, published January 25, 2019.

101 Ibid.

102 Ibid.

China. Within this unfriendly environment, *danwei* seems to offer a sanctuary for its female employees with its egalitarian principles. The competitive labor market demands unwavering dedications from employees to their careers, often forcing them to work extremely long hours from early morning to late night. Children's education also demands attention and care from their mothers. Confronted with growing pressure and irreconcilable conflicts between their career and family, more Chinese women are choosing to leave their intensive careers behind in order to dedicate more time to their families.

Taking care of children is not an easy task. This responsibility not only keeps millions of mothers busy and preoccupied but also compels many to abandon their career to revolve themselves around their children. Unfortunately, this also deprives many women of opportunities to engage and participate within the society in meaningful ways. Many stay-at-home mothers often found themselves disconnected from the society around them, interacting only with mothers of similar backgrounds and their husbands and children.

DANWEI TO THE RESCUE?

As the director of a district Women's Federation at Hefei, Mrs. He (who happens to have the same last name as I do), has witnessed the plight shared by many stay-at-home mothers in China. "They want to reconnect with society, but they don't know how." In the name of sacrificing for the family and for future generations, many mothers have forfeited not only their careers, but also their hobbies, their friends, and their very identity as women. In Mrs. He's words, the crisis moment occurred for many when they lost their independent identity and became affiliates of their children. They were no longer addressed by their name, but as mothers of their children. The solution, for Mrs. He, is the *danwei* system, which enables employees to grow their careers while raising their children. "A *danwei* career offers stability and flexibility...no one will punish you for devoting more time to family rather than work...and whenever you are ready to jump back to work again, the opportunity is always there."

Many women I interviewed substantiated Mrs. He's claims and were highly satisfied with their current arrangement. Mrs. Chen, for example, enjoyed the flexibility to leave work in the event that a family emergency occurs. In her workplace, she can switch between work and family seamlessly without anyone questioning her commitment. For Mrs. Chen and others like her who have, in her words, "no aspiration to rise through the ranks and make a name for [herself]," the *danwei* career offers work-life balance.

Mrs. Chen is content with what she has as a public servant, but why do women like her have to make the sacrifice? Where are their husbands when someone needs to drive their children to school? Where are their husbands when their parent got sick? Where are their husbands when someone needs to cook and clean the house? A closer look at this arrangement reveals the unfortunate fact that the *danwei* career offers no solution, but simply a diversion, to the larger problem at stake. For millions of women in China, the essential issue is not the difficulty of balancing between work and family, but the very expectation that they must reach for such a balance whereas their husbands do not. In other words, a *danwei* career is not necessarily beneficial for women, but for wives and mothers expected to devote themselves to take care of the family. In fact, it is not uncommon to encounter parents urging their daughters to become public servants and have "stable careers," be it in real life or television shows.

The popular Chinese television drama *Nothing But Thirty* follows three thirty-something-year-old women though unprecedented obstacles in marriage, education, and career. In a recent episode, the character Wang Manni's story as a sales-clerk of a high-end fashion designer store who left her home-town to seek better opportunities in Shanghai resonated with many among the audience. Besides challenges in her career path and difficulties with her romantic encounters, Wang Manni also faces pressures from her small-town parents, who urge her to quit fighting monsters alone in Shanghai as an outsider, return home to settle down with a reputable *danwei* desk job, and marry a local government official.

A stable *danwei* career has attracted thousands of male and female applicants, but its benefits differ between the two genders. *Danwei* offers a sense of security in the current highly competitive labor market, but the flexibility of commitment benefits primarily female employees. The path to promotion for male employees includes an expectation to voluntarily put in extra hours without overtime pay. Many parents encourage their sons to have a *danwei* career because of the reputation and stability, but they encourage their daughters to do the same so they can devote more time to the family. From this perspective, the *danwei* society resembles not a symbol of egalitarianism and gender equality, but another embodiment of the patriarchal order and the deep-rooted gender inequality in China.

Domestic gender inequality is not a new topic in China, but many have yet to acknowledge the *danwei* system's role in perpetuating those traditional values. Even when recent feminist movements challenge the traditional notion that assigns the domestic sphere to the responsibility of women, many do not see the *danwei* system as particularly problematic. Instead, many join Mrs. He in believing a *danwei* career liberates women from the suffocating dual burden of work and family. Explaining the prevalence of such belief, Mrs. He pointed out that at the district, county, or township levels, female public servants outnumber their male counterparts. The fairer hiring process partially accounts for this gender composition, but another important reason is that "men of similar or equal skills and qualifications usually seek more challenging and better paying positions at higher levels and in large cities such as Beijing and Shanghai." In this traditional belief, adventurism belongs to men and women should happily prioritize stability.

As women are becoming more equal to men in China in terms of education attainment and economic contribution, they are still discouraged to strive for excellence the same way their male counterparts are. In 2015, Chinese women contributed 41 percent to the national GDP, a higher percentage than in most other regions worldwide, including Western Europe and North America.[103] Women's active role in the

103 Peter Vanham, "Women in China Contribute More to GDP than in the US. Viewing Them as 'Leftover' is Problematic," World Economic Forum, published April 12, 2018.

consumption market, especially via e-commerce platforms such as Taobao and JD, has also given rise to a new phenomenon known as the "she economy (她经济)," reflecting the emergence of an economic sector serving and catering to the needs of women. Women's success in the economy, however, has yet to translate to liberation from the limitations imposed by traditional gender dynamics.

Within this environment, the *danwei* system plays a crucial though not necessarily intentional role in perpetuating and reinforcing the current unequal gender dynamics. Though it offers a solution for women squeezed between work and family, it also creates a social expectation that significantly limits the aspiration of thousands of women in China. Women are encouraged and expected to follow a nine-to-five work schedule and prioritize family over work whenever demanded.

Seven decades since the first call to liberate women from the burden of feudalism, the quest for equality remains far from over. Chinese citizens, especially younger generations, are indeed becoming more socially progressive on issues including gender inequality. Unfortunately, many of the institutions once designed to showcase the promise of egalitarianism no longer shine as beacons for greater equality. The *danwei* system, ironically, has fallen as an accomplice to traditional values. It has become an institution sustaining and perpetuating the discriminatory notion of separated spheres, rather than shattering the chains of feudal ideals and protecting women from the unjustified discriminations ubiquitous in the private sector.

PART FIVE

DREAM OR ILLUSION

人民对美好生活的向往，就是我们的奋斗目标

习近平　2012年11月15日同中外记者讲话

People's yearning for a beautiful life
is the goal of our endeavors.

XI JINPING WHEN SPEAKING TO
JOURNALISTS ON NOVEMBER 15, 2012

CHAPTER 11

ANOTHER ANGLE OF CHINA'S SUCCESS STORY

———

I don't make it back to Hefei frequently enough to stay abreast of economic development there. The city's changing so quickly that when I fly home once or twice a year, it feels like landing in the middle of a surprise party.

Every time I return to my hometown, my parents take me on a tour of the city's new developments, pointing out buildings I have not seen before and telling me big news stories that happened while I was away. I've now been away for eight years and those economic development tours have become a treasured family tradition.

When I flew into Hefei in the winter of 2016, the city greeted me with the biggest surprise of all. I'd known for years of plans to construct a metro rail system in Hefei. I also knew that train cars filled with commuters would traverse the rails that lay deep beneath my family's apartment. But I did not expect to participate in the event that redefined Hefei. Throughout the winter break, everyone around me was talking about the new metro and an air of excitement and jubilation floated in the city. It was the day after Christmas and the new stations were as clean and bright as new-fallen snow. On the track, pristine red and white paint made an empty passenger car look like it had just been unwrapped and removed from its package. After the initial craze faded, I went for a ride in the middle of the day while most people were at work. Sitting in the empty train, I wondered if this was an epitome of China's success story.

I commenced my study on public servants in China to understand how Chinese citizens are engaging with the idea of the Chinese Dream. My mother has worked as a lower-level public servant for over three decades, so even before I did any research on this topic, I already had a general idea as to what a career in public service entails. But if my mother's story has given me any clue to my question, it is that there is no straight answer to it. Depending on which perspective I adopt, I shall draw different conclusions. Compared to my father's work as a manager in a private company, my mother's career represents a completely different reality. She rarely works late, seldomly discusses job stress, and never brings work tasks home with her. Before I could understand the concept of the *iron rice bowl*, I already knew that while her indifferent attitude would not award her a raise or promotion, my mother never feared a demotion or dismissal. At the same time, my mother made no secret that she earned considerably less than my father and her peers in the private sector.

PESSIMISTIC YOUTH

For one month, I conducted interviews and participant observation at several work units at Hefei. As it turns out, the economic angle is only one among many facets worth exploring. In Chinese unique social and historical context, the work unit is far more than merely a place of work. Though *danwei* no longer maintains the powerful authority over its employees as the intermediary between the state and the individuals, it still commands substantial influence and prestige as a term synonymous to the government. Public servants thus enjoy much greater social, political, and symbolic capital simply by the affiliation with their *danwei*.

Many of the privileges exclusive to a *danwei* career also serve as sources of dissatisfaction and disillusionment shared by many as the system encourages hierarchy, uniformity, and rigidity. To further complicate this duality of privilege and control, the *danwei* environment embodies a distinct set of reality depending on one's age and gender. While the significant roles age and gender play in how one perceives and rationalizes the career of public service should not come as a surprise given the relevance of the two factors in research on social attitudes, I nevertheless invite you to delve deeper in this and the subsequent chapter by asking why these two differences matter and what they tell us about the Chinese society.

To understand how age impacts a population's attitudes or behavior, researchers have to distinguish between the age effect and the cohort effect.[104] An age or aging effect is a change in the value of the dependent or explained variable which occurs among the entire population independently of the time period as everyone grows older. A cohort effect models the change that characterizes the group of people born at a particular time period and thus independent of the aging process.

One may observe that younger people are more politically progressive than older generations and ascribe it to either aging or the cohort effect. Proponents of the former will argue that as people age, they become more risk averse. A forty-year-old middle manager with two children has more to lose than a college student if both get arrested after participating in a protest. Advocates for the cohort effects would make the case that young people today are more progressive because they grow up in a more progressive era than their parents and grandparents. The rise of the internet and social media enabled many previously hidden, oppressed, or overlooked voices to speak out against the injustices and problems in the society, convincing many young people to take personal interests and make commitments to the more progressive agenda.

It is evident the public servants of different ages perceive their career environment very differently. Mrs. Zhu's comment on many among today's youth lacking her generation's adventurous and entrepreneurial spirits is a telling account

---

104 John Hobcraft, Jane Menken, and Samuel Preston, "Age, Period, and Cohort Effects in Demography: A Review," in *Cohort Analysis in Social Research*, ed. William M. Mason and Stephen E. Fienberg (New York: Springer, 1985), 89-135.

on how age, or more specifically, birth cohort, matters when talking about public servants in China.

Birth cohort exists beyond academic studies. Western countries have long categorized people into different demographic groups such as Baby Boomers for babies born between the mid 1940s to the mid 1960s. China adopts a different system, marking the beginning of a new decade as the start of a new generation. People born between 1960 and 1970 are known as the *60-hou* (after 1960) and those born between 1990 and 2000 are called the *90-hou* (after 1990). Using this popular rule as a guide, I propose to divide the current *danwei* employees into two groups, the *6070-hou* and the *8090-hou*, where the former roughly represents the more senior employees and the latter denotes the younger ones. This categorization is interesting and important for many reasons.

The *6070-hou* share similar upbringings. They grew up around the time of the Cultural Revolution. They also witnessed or experienced the Tiananmen Massacre during their adolescent or early adult years. *8090-hou* grew up in a new era without the terror of war, famine, or radical movements. As the first two post-reform generations, they are modern, tech-savvy, and open-minded. Born during the height of the one-child policy, they have earned the reputation of being rebellious, individualistic, and self-centered.

In the mind of most *6070-hou*, *8090-hou* is a "generation growing up inside honey jars (蜜罐里长大的一代)." A *90-hou* myself, I grew up believing the "honey jars" metaphor referred to the convenience of technological advancement. With easy access to the internet, I can look up any information in ways my parents and grandparents could never have imagined during their adolescent years. Soon I realized the "honey jar" was much more than that. *8090-hou* was the first generation in over a century to grow up in a time of peace, free from the fear of war and famine endured by their grandparents and the devastations of political purges and the Cultural Revolution that carved into the memories of their parents.

The generation divide cuts even further in the *danwei* environment. The commercialization of the housing market in the late 1990s means many *6070-hou* received substantial housing benefits and subsidies from their work units. Most *8090-hou*, however, missed the last train of cheap, affordable housing and face very difficult financial conditions on their path to homeownership against ballooning housing prices.

Influenced by their unique experience in the early reform era, many senior public servants view younger colleagues in a rather negative and pessimistic light. To accept Mrs. Zhu's characterization that young people today in general lack adventurous spirits and tenacity would do the current youth a great disservice and grossly ignores the achievements of many young Chinese entrepreneurs clustered in Beijing and Shanghai. At the same time, it is equally problematic to completely dismiss Mrs. Zhu's observation. After all, millions of university graduates in China are lining up for a *danwei* career known for its strict hierarchy and rigidity.

There is an overwhelming belief in China that the nation will continue to deliver rapid economic growth. The government has also repeatedly called on university graduates to demonstrate their entrepreneurial spirits. Why, then, are so many young people in China willing to settle for complacency?

Chinese youths are not pessimistic toward China's bright future. Most young *danwei* employees I interviewed took tremendous pride in China's economic performance despite recent economic slowdown. Nor do they lack the ambition and aspiration that once drove *6070-hou* to embrace the newly developed free market. They are complacent because they have to be. Driven by a deep sense of resignation and helplessness, many opt for guaranteed complacency rather than facing the uncertain and unwelcoming world with unrealistic promise of success.

PARADISE LOST

To understand this inveterate pessimism among many well-educated youths in China, I borrow the thesis of "compressed development" proposed and developed by Hugh Whittaker et al.[105] Observing "the simultaneity of high and low development indicators"—such as the presence of both primitive machine tools and advanced computer-controlled machining centers in the same factory in China and Taiwan— Whittaker et al developed a new compressed development model. This new model of development differs from the "late development" model that described the rapid industrialization and economic development in countries such as Japan.[106]

---

105 D. Hugh Whittaker et al, "Compressed Development," *Studies in Comparative International Development* 45 (2010): 439-467.
106 Ibid, 440.

A key difference between the compressed development model and earlier models of development is the timeframe of industrialization and the extent of compression. Whereas development unfolded over more than a century in the UK and around fifty years in Japan, the same process has been compressed into ever shorter periods for more recent developers such as South Korea, Taiwan, and China. In China's case especially, the consequence of compressed development is obvious. Factories often introduce advanced production machines so quickly that they have not had the time to disassemble and throw out more primitive equipment.

Moreover, the compression of development timeline also has impacts on social structures and institutions that take much longer to evolve and adapt. The rush toward industrialization and modernity furthers the value divide between the urban workers and rural farmers and between senior citizens and the youth:

> *The social relations and values commonly associated with agricultural or early industrial societies—a high value placed on male children, for instance—can overlap with late or post-industrial emphases on equality and better educational opportunities for women, exacerbating gender tensions and accelerating trends towards later marriage, declining childbirth rates and societal ageing that typically come with later stages of economic development.*[107]

---

107 Ibid.

At the same time, institutions, be it financial, legal, or educational, are under severe pressure to evolve and adapt for countries undergoing compressed development. The rise and expansion of the middle class brought by economic development frequently led to greater popular demand for social and political changes such as democratization, government accountability, and greater equality. Movements pushing for political reform occurred in China, South Korea, and Taiwan, though in China's case the party-state was able to suppress such popular demand and maintain one-party authoritarian rule. Rapid industrialization and urbanization also created a myriad of problems and conflicts from environmental degradation to worsening social inequality that need fundamental institutional changes. Whereas countries such as the US and the UK had a longer time frame to adjust, adapt, and experiment, time is an extremely scarce resource for many newly industrialized countries.

Another helpful tool to solve our puzzle is the demographic transition model, which traces population changes throughout history and proposes five stages of population growth.[108] By observing the change in birth and death rate throughout history, the demographic transition theory proposes a negative correlation between industrialization and birth rate. As countries evolve from pre-industrial societies characterized by high birth rate and high mortality rate to post-industrial states of low birth rate and low death rate, death rate declines prior to falling birth rate, creating a demographic window or

---

108 Frank W. Notestein et al., *The Future Population of Europe and the Soviet Union: Population Projections, 1940-1970* (Geneva: League of Nations, 1944).

demographic dividend that supports and facilitates economic development.

In China's case, its demographic transition does not follow a typical trajectory as in the classical model. Years of wars, famines, and domestic turmoil contributed to extremely high death rates, which did not decline significantly until the 1960s. Following the decline of the death rate, birth rate also fell rapidly as the state implemented the one-child policy, restricting most families in China to one child. The dramatic change in China's demographic composition created a short yet significant demographic dividend as the working age population expanded in the 1990s and 2000s while the number of dependents, especially children, declined in each household.

China completed its demographic transition by the early 2000s. The steady trend of low birth rate and low death rate also marked the end of the era of demographic window. For *6070-hou*, the 1990s to early 2000s was an economic golden age. Not only did new waves of economic reform present unprecedented opportunities, but declining birth rate also meant less burden on child rearing and greater accumulation of personal wealth. The *8090-hou*, on the other hand, face a different reality. Though the economy continues to expand and the standard of living rises steadily, young people appear more worried and less secure than previous generations. A telling story is China's steady low birth rate even after the government lifted the one-child policy. Birth rate in urban areas, especially highly developed metropolises, remains abysmal. Moreover, even with just one child to take care of, most *8090-hou* already and will face more pressure than

6070-hou since the burden of elderly care cannot be shared among siblings.

To add to the stress and dilemma many young people face today from a demographic perspective, the rapid economic growth in China under the compressed development model has failed to create equal opportunity for all. Recalling the striking expansion of high education in the 1990s discussed in previous chapters, the value of a university degree has depreciated significantly in recent years. The number of college graduates has increased significantly, but opportunities for skilled, well-paid positions have not expanded as much. Thus while graduates from top-tier universities have little problem finding a satisfactory job, less qualified but nevertheless well-educated youths are left behind.

Against the depreciation of higher education is the long-held expectation that education changes destiny. Success stories of university graduates in the early days of the economic reform supported this Confucian teaching, but the current environment seems to refute this ancient wisdom. To further exacerbate this dashing expectation, China's economic growth is driven primarily by low value-added manufacturing activities, not research and development (R&D). Opportunities for low-skilled labors, however, do not apply to college graduates especially when the Chinese society discriminates against blue-collar workers as uneducated and even boorish.

Finally, rising living cost across urban China adds even more burden to the already tenuous financial conditions of many young people in China. Mr. Chen's path toward homeownership mentioned in chapter six is a common, if not normal practice in China. Most parents, even ones who are not financially well-to-do, will contribute the down payment if not the entire cost of the apartment for their children. Even with parental support, mortgage itself still poses a heavy burden for many young people in China.

While China's skyrocketing real estate price is no longer foreign news for many inside and outside China, it is nevertheless useful to put it in comparative perspective. Given the average housing price in Hefei, which stands at around 15,000 RMB per square meter ($200 per square foot), the value of a 100-square meter apartment in Hefei is equivalent to a condo roughly the same size near Washington, DC, or a much more spacious house in Baltimore.[109] Yet housing is only the first challenge among many. The depreciation of university education in general has not compelled the government to systematically reform the education system. It has convinced most parents to spend more time and money making sure their children can go to the best university possible. A news report published in 2016 ranked the top ten most expensive cities in China to raise a child. Beijing tops the chart with 2.76 billion RMB ($413,000).[110]

Chang Chun, a second-tiered city with similar GDP as Hefei as of 2018, ranked 10 with 1.35 billion RMB ($202,000).[111] If we take this number for Hefei today, which is likely lower

109 Data collected from several online real estate marketplace companies, such as Anjuke (安居客) in China and Zillow in the US, offering insights on market trends.
110 "养孩成本TOP10城市曝光: 养个孩子消灭一个百万富翁 (Top 10 Cities by Cost of Raising a Child: Raising a Child Can Destroy a Millionaire)," *Southern Metropolis Daily*, September 20, 2016.
111 Ibid.

than the actual cost, it would take a family of two public servants eighteen years and nine months to save this much money, assuming both parents earn 10,000 RMB per month and save 30 percent of their income.

One could easily cast pessimistic labels on today's youth. Before we write them off as a complacent, lost, or spoiled generation, we must keep in mind that each generation's attitudes and behaviors reflect the environment they grew up in. Their apathetic and pessimistic attitude toward their future reflects an interplay between their expectation of a bright future and a cold, unwelcoming reality. In many ways, their lives are defined by a sense of paradox. By official definition, they are certainly living in moderate prosperity because they are well above the poverty line and enjoy a comfortable lifestyle. At the same time, however, their constant fears and worries cast doubt on such conclusion.

One may counter my reservation by pointing out that pessimistic youth is also not an exclusively Chinese phenomenon. Young people in many developed countries such as Japan face similar challenges that result in low birth rate and a culture of resignation. This counterargument is valid, but China's case is different because whereas most developed nations face economic stagnation or slow recovery, China is still booming. While Beijing's economic performance has instilled a sense of pride in the hearts of many young people in China, it has not brought a strong sense of optimism. "Moderate prosperity" is not merely an economic benchmark; it should also reflect an optimistic and confident state of mind. From this perspective, young Chinese public servants may be moderately prosperous on paper, but not in their actions and attitudes.

CHAPTER 12

WHO FAILED WHOM?

———

In the summer of 2020, I—like most of the world—was self-quarantining. From a half-basement near Georgetown in Washington, DC, I phoned a friend in China, eager to share my news: I'd decided to put my research, thoughts, and insights on China's public servants into a book.

Before we knew it, our discussion had drifted from the feasibility of the book to the many social problems I planned to address in this book. Halfway through our conversation, he asked me my thoughts on involution (内卷), a new term that has gained tremendous popularity recently. I had no idea what he was even talking about. Embarrassed by my unfamiliarity, I turned to social media to see if anyone happened to have mentioned the term in their posts. And judging by the frequency and volume of #involution mentions, it seemed I might have been the only Chinese who had no idea what my friend was talking about.

After reading through popular discussions of involution on Chinese social media, I soon realized while the term only gained popularity in 2020, the underlying problems have existed for decades and intensified in recent years.

Upon hearing involution (内卷) in Chinese for the first time, I assumed the term is a neologism describing the motion of curling toward the inside, which is the direct translation of 内卷. Ironically, the English translation helped me locate its source, a famous work by Clifford Geertz titled *Agricultural Involution: The Process of Ecological Change in Indonesia*. Studying the agricultural system in Indonesia, Geertz observed the intensification of rice cultivation due to external demand and internal pressure, leading to growing complexity without significant technological breakthrough or political reform, a phenomenon he termed "agricultural involution."[112]

In *The Peasant Economy and Social Change in North China*, sociologist Philip Huang introduced the concept "agricultural involution" to Chinese scholars. Since then, sociologists in China have expanded this concept of increasing intensification without breakthrough beyond rural studies.[113] In 2020, involution gained further recognition in China when it walked into the eyes of the general public and has become one of the most referenced terms since. There have been talks about involution in the workplace, in universities, and most shockingly, in kindergartens.[114]

---

112 Clifford Geertz, *Agricultural Involution: The Processes of Ecological Change in Indonesia* (Berkeley: University of California Press, 1969).

113 See Phillip C. C. Huang, *The Peasant Economy and Social Change in North China* (Stanford: Stanford University Press, 1988) and Prasenjit Duara, *Culture, Power, and the State: Rural North China, 1900–1942* (Stanford: Stanford University Press, 1998).

114 "2020年十大流行语揭晓 (Ten Most Popular Phrases in 2020)," *People's Daily*, December 5, 2020.

INVOLUTION WITH CHINESE CHARACTERISTICS

So what does involution look like in China?

On university campuses, where the term first became famous, involution is embodied in the famous photo depicting a student holding a laptop in his palm while riding his bike on campus.[115] Though the student caught in the photo later explained he was only making sure his program kept running without interruption, his fellow classmates were not surprised by his action. In fact, multitasking—from eating while riding a bike to staring at laptop screens while eating lunch—is an experience shared by many university students in China.[116] Endless competition is more conspicuous inside classrooms, where students submit twenty-page essays for an assignment requiring ten pages to receive an "A." This tactic may work once or twice, but as soon as everyone else follows suit, the bar to success increases and competition intensifies.

For those feeling the effect of involution, it means a sense of physical and mental exhaustion from burning out. It means the disillusionment of endlessly competing for advancement without making anything more than marginal progress. It resembles the economic concept of diminishing marginal return, which describes the phenomenon of rapid decreases in the marginal output when the amount of labor increases after an optimal point. In China, people feel they have gone way past the optimal equilibrium. Putting in more efforts

---

115 "清华学生边骑车边用电脑？当事人：因害怕关闭机盖程序中断 (Tsinghua Student Using Laptop While Riding Bike? Student Claims Afraid of Program Interruption)," *The Paper*, September 30, 2020.

116 Ibid.

does not guarantee one equal, or even marginal return, but merely maintaining the status quo is already a luxury.

For parents, it is the intense pressure to provide the best resources for their children, often spending an unimaginable amount of time, energy, and money on education. For children, it means trying to keep up in the rat race for the best educational resources, which often requires them to sacrifice their childhoods and behave twice or three times their age. For office workers, it means locked in their office cell for hours with no end in sight. Needless to say, the world of involution is dark and dull, resembling an iron cage mentioned in previous chapters the Chinese people had once rid themselves of in the late 1970s.

GENIUSES AT FOUR: A BLUEPRINT FOR SUCCESS

Take involution in kindergartens as an example. In 2020, a series of news stories of elementary school children committing suicide shocked Chinese society. On April 13, a twelve-year-old girl jumped out of a building on the first day of school. A month later, a nine-year old girl jumped out of a fifth-floor apartment after leaving her parents a scribbled note: "Why can't I do anything well (为什么我干什么都不行)."[117]

While China mourned for the loss of these young, innocent lives, intense competition starting as early as kindergarten did not pause for a second.

---

117 "幼儿园已经开始内卷了 (Involution Has Begun in Kindergartens)," *The Paper,* October 14, 2020.

In Shanghai and Beijing, getting into a top kindergarten marks a significant challenge for most families. Attending these elite kindergartens not only requires a strong family background but also good timing and a fair amount of luck. Most of these kindergartens boast advanced education systems and models imported from abroad. To uphold their elite standard, they open their doors only to a select few. Tuitions at these schools cost at least 10,000 RMB ($1,546) per month. The admission process not only tests the aptitude of the prospective student but may also subject their parents to an interview.[118]

Even after this pre-admission selection rules out most middle-class families, competition for these elite kindergartens remains unimaginably competitive. For kindergartens with pre-K (托班) programs, securing a spot at the affiliated pre-K school is almost a requirement for admission. For those that do not, the real application process begins just as early. Months and years before sending their children off to kindergarten, parents already sign up to endless waiting lists hoping to receive a chance for an interview. In 2020, for example, Shanghai's Victoria Kindergarten had an acceptance rate of barely 1.3 percent, or one acceptance among every seventy-five applicants.[119] Other kindergartens, such as the Montessori School of Shanghai, required parents to sign up to waiting lists at least a year prior to admission. At the most sought-after school—Jiabao Kindergarten in Shanghai—the acceptance rate approached impossibility. By one account, parents who dream of sending their future

118 Ibid.
119 "上海10所最热门私立幼儿园！ (Top 10 Private Kindergartens in Shanghai! Preparing)," *Sohu News*, August 17, 2018.

three-year-old to the elite kindergarten had better start preparing early—perhaps as early as the third trimester. One parent revealed that when she initiated the application process for her young child, a school representative informed her she was too late to secure a spot. At the time, her future kindergartener was only three days old.[120]

What factors make these elite kindergartens special?

A cursory look at their websites may lead to the conclusion they have more resources, more advanced education concepts, and better-trained faculty.[121] Indeed, compared to public or non-elite private kindergartens, these elite preschools house incredible resources, from foreign teachers, specially designed class structures and textbooks, immersive multilingual environment, and sometimes, unmatched facilities such as ice rinks. More important for parents, these elite kindergartens are feeder schools for the best primary schools in Beijing and Shanghai, and the hierarchy reaches up to the very best universities in the country.

Although attending the best preschools significantly increases one's chance to advance through the best education system in China, it does not guarantee a path of success. Competition within these schools remains extremely intense. This air of heightened competition has led to a popular practice called "鸡娃" in China, which is short for "给孩子打鸡血," literally

---

120 "出生就要排队！上海10所热门幼儿园青浦独占其3，入园攻略曝光！(Waiting in Line Since the Day of Birth! Top 10 Private Kindergartens in Shanghai and the How to Guide)," *Tencent News*, March 10, 2020.

121 Most of these private elite kindergartens highlighted these attributes as their strengthens on their official websites.

translating to "using chicken-blood therapy on children."[122] Chicken-blood therapy refers to a form of pseudo-medical therapy popular in China during the Cultural Revolution. In practice, it involved injecting rooster blood into patients with the intention of making them strong and aggressive. In the contemporary context, chicken-blood therapy no longer refers to the pseudo-scientific practice. Today, the term denotes using external stimuli to make someone excited or motivated. To use chicken-blood therapy on children, parents are no longer satisfied with what is taught at school. They fill their children's schedules with complementary classes, tutoring sessions, and training for extracurricular activities.

Despite being called complementary classes (补习班), these after-school sessions are rarely a means of consolidating knowledge learned inside classrooms or providing language training appropriate to children's ages. Instructors teach middle school physics to eight-year-olds or expecting kindergarten children to be polymaths and prodigies. These complementary classes are not exclusive to only elites in Beijing and Shanghai. Middle-class households are also avid participants within this rat race for excellence.[123]

Within this highly competitive environment, claiming expertise can hardly convince anyone. Contests and exams have naturally become the primary platform to showcase one's skills. The most common include music exams (考级), subject-specific Olympiad contests, and the Science & Technology Innovation Contest. Parents of piano or violin

---

122 "真的要把孩子变成 '鸡娃' 吗? (Should We Really Use 'Chicken Blood Therapy' on Children?)," *Xinhua News*, December 16, 2019.
123 Ibid.

learners want their children to pass the practical grade 8 exam offered by the Associated Board of the Royal Schools of Music (ABRM) in England. Parents with children studying for math, computer science, or physics Olympiad hope for a provincial or national award. For most students, winning an award is not only a sign of competence but also a golden ticket in the race for top universities as special recruits.

As the race for excellence becomes increasingly competitive, so is it becoming more out of control. In 2020, a sixth grader from Kunming won third prize at the China Adolescents Science & Technology Innovation Contest with a project on the "research on the function and role of C10orf67 in the development of colon cancer." If C10orf67 sounds unfamiliar, do not worry. Most people, perhaps save medical students and this sixth-grade prodigy, can hardly understand the research design, much less how to actually conduct this research. Online, the news of this young prodigy was received with skepticism. Medical students either questioned the feasibility of the research or praised the sixth grader with sarcasm.[124] The public commented on the teenager's research journal, which documented his transformation from not knowing what a gene is to conducting rigorous research with advanced equipment within weeks.[125]

124 "小学生研究癌症相关基因或将被质疑造假 (Primary School Students Who Won Awards for Research on Cancer-Related Genes Questioned for Forgery)" *Lianhe Zaobao*, July 17, 2020.

125 "小学生研究基因与癌症关系拿大奖，5天学会专业知识，水平堪比博士！父母身份曝光... (Primary School Student Won Big Prize with Research on the Cancer and Gene. Mastered Expertise in Five Days Rivaling PhDs)," *National Business Daily*, July 13, 2020.

Kunming Animal Research Institute later announced the student had direct relatives to researchers at the institute and promised to investigate the matter. The controversies, however, remained unsettled as to whether such research was fair or independent. A cursory look at the other award-winning projects reveals the problem is not limited to a few singular incidents. Many research topics can easily qualify for a graduate-level research paper and require strong field expertise and at times advanced equipment. More importantly, some of the research topics are simply "too boring" for primary school students.[126]

Using personal connections and personal research results to decorate the experience and knowledge of their children is only one way for parents to make their children more competitive. For most families, the key to success is not crediting their teenagers as first authors but pushing their children to the limit, and within China, no parents do it better than moms in Haidian and Shunyi districts in Beijing. To not waste a minute of their children's time, many mothers in Haidian and Shunyi have opted for a career as stay-at-home mothers, planning out every minute and every detail for their children. On weekends and during breaks, they drive their children to complementary classes, art lessons, and sports practices. When these complementary classes are in session, they either take notes quietly in the back so they can tutor their children later or chat with fellow mothers to catch up with recent trends in education. As the pioneer among

126 "青少年科技创新大赛充斥着大量研究癌症、基因、细菌的中小学生 (Youth Innovation Competition Filled with Primary and Middle School Students Researching Cancer, Genes, and Bacteria)," *NetEast News*, July 21, 2020.

millions of parents in China, these mothers are extremely knowledgeable of the best educational resources available and how to acquire them. At the moment, that means sending their children abroad as early as possible to aim for a bachelor's degree from an Ivy League colleague in the US or Oxbridge in the UK.[127]

As competition for studying abroad becomes more intense, what constitutes a good application for prospective students in China has changed significantly in the past decade. In the early 2010s, before and around the time I applied to high schools in the US, TOEFL and SSAT scores were two of the most important factors. Almost everyone around me invested a large portion of their time in standardized tests. Extracurricular activities from sports and music talents to volunteer experience matter but were not viewed as decisive elements. In recent years, this perception has shifted significantly. I felt it during my college application process in 2016 and 2017. By then, most applicants—at least most applying to top-tiered schools in the US—had near-perfect TOEFL and SAT scores. What was once an achievement worth celebrating has now become almost a bare requirement. In the competition for Ivy League schools, essays and experience became more important. To refurbish their resume, many applicants signed up for short-term activities, especially volunteer trips, to show both a commitment to justice and an interest to explore and immerse in other cultures.

---

127 "海淀家长和顺义妈妈的鸡娃史，一场父母的集体焦虑，如何破解困局 (The History of Haidian Parents and Shunyi Moms, A Collective Anxiety Among Chinese Parents)," *NetEast News*, September 16, 2020.

Not only are US universities becoming more competitive for Chinese applicants, but the competition has also expanded down to US high schools. To prepare for increasing challenges in advance, many parents train their children to excel at a common and traditional weak point among Chinese applicants—sports. Given the general focus on studying and the perception that equates sports with play and leisure activities, Chinese students have rarely been good students and active athletes at the same time. But with more parents realizing this gap is worth exploring, sports have regained interest among Chinese elites. The resurgent attention to sports also served to showcase class and status. Sports that have already established a strong presence in the country, from badminton and ping-pong to basketball and volleyball, are not looked down upon but certainly have less appeal than more exotic options such as ice hockey, equestrian, and polo.

On the surface, the intense competition within China's education system, starting from kindergarten in metropolises such as Beijing and Shanghai, seems crazy and out of control, but the logic behind it is intuitive. The scarcity of education resources and the singular criterion for selection—academic excellence—determines that the paths toward good universities are highly unequal. Students in Beijing and Shanghai already have higher chances to get into top-tiered universities than their peers from other backgrounds, and among them, graduates of top high schools are more likely to win the race. This leads to a chain of feeder schools, from high schools down to kindergartens. And this phenomenon does not exist in Shanghai and Beijing alone. In Hefei, for example, No. 1, No. 8, and No. 6 high schools—especially the first two—are widely recognized as the top three. While all students have an equal chance to attend, better middle schools—No. 45 (where I attended), No. 42, No. 48, and No. 50—send more students every year. Thus while one does not have to graduate from one of the four middle schools to secure enrollment at the top three high schools, doing so increases one's chances significantly. In Hefei, the competition seeps down to the primary school level but less so among kindergartens. The more developed an area is, the earlier the competition begins. Where there is intensive competition, there is involution (内卷).

THERE'S NO WAY OUT: EDUCATED MEDIOCRACY

Unlike children who often experience involution from the pressure exerted by their parents, college students and young *danwei* employees I interviewed face involution from a diverse range of sources, including their peers, family, and society. In a state of involution, as described earlier, hard work does not necessarily yield comparable results because others work just as hard, regardless of whether they have better starting positions or not. Being in a state of involution is thus comparable to being a hamster in a wheel with a dozen others. There is no option save to run as fast as the others. Running a bit faster does not yield any benefit but may only hurt as you climb up and ultimately fall.

This air of pessimism is also reflected in another word that gained popularity in 2020—laborer (打工人). Though the origin of the word as uttered by a construction worker on his TikTok (抖音) account was not meant to be used sarcastically, the term soon became popular among Chinese youths to express a sense of defeatism and a lack of control of their own destinies.[128] While the term had yet to become an internet buzzword by the time I conducted my interview, a similar air of pessimism doomed on many young *danwei* employees I interviewed as many felt trapped in a sense of failure. This sense of failure is two sided. They feel failed by the society and by the promise of a bright future when they felt the disillusionment of reality. At the same time, they are often forced to accept they have in fact failed the system because they are not smart, diligent, or adventurous enough to grasp the opportunity that is available to all.

So who failed whom?

The answer is certainly more complicated than simply saying one is right and the other is wrong. Over the past four decades, average Chinese citizens certainly have had greater chances to succeed than previous generations and I standby that belief because I am one of the lucky few. But greater opportunity does not mean equality. The system has failed many because for many the promise of success is only a mirage.

I believe the root of the problem lies in China's education system. The rat race for what constitutes success begins as early as kindergarten, and for many who graduate from college believing they have done it, post-graduation reality only tells them to rethink everything they have ever known.

---

128 Wang Xuandi, "Socially Dead Laborers of Versailles: China's 2020 in Memes," Sixth Tone, published December 11, 2020.

A major issue with China's education system is the accurate analogy of the single-plank bridge of *gaokao* (高考), or the college entrance exam. Similar to the SAT, *gaokao* is a standardized test measuring the aptitude of a student on several subjects, including Chinese, math, English, and comprehensive science subjects. Depending on whether a student chooses to pursue natural science or social science in high school, the comprehensive science portion differs between physics, chemistry, and biology for the former and history, geology, and political science for the latter. Unlike the SAT, however, *gaokao* can be taken only once a year and weighs 100 percent in the university application process unless one can demonstrate special talents. Just as critics of the SAT have claimed standardized tests are too rigid to test the actual capability of a student, *gaokao* faces similar criticisms, but its defendants, including many senior *danwei* I interviewed, still see its values in "creating a leveled playing field."

While *gaokao* is certainly part of the problem, I see the root lies deeper than the mechanisms employed in the education system. The rigidity of the system is merely a reflection of the rigidity of popular belief and perception. Competition is endless and becomes increasingly intense because in the market of success, demand always outweighs success, and as more Chinese are being educated each year, the gap only widens. Instead of trying to alter the mechanism that runs this invisible market, why not change the supply side of the equation? So many Chinese youths believe they are failures because Chinese society condones an extremely narrow definition of success. Thus many-middle class families are engaged in the frenzy rat race not because they seek to climb upward but to ensure their children do not fall. Within this environment, involution occurs not because of the population size or the lack of resources, but because of the artificial limits set on the optimum number of successes allowed.

I asked my interviewees to describe their visions of success. Their responses do not differ significantly from what I expected or heard from my American peers. What is puzzling is the idea that the path to that success is singular. People may respect athletes who win Olympic gold medals, but such is not the optimal path toward success. Many dream to become celebrities in movies but acting is not the optimal path. In the contemporary world, the ancient wisdom that "one may distinguish himself in any trade (行行出状元)" seems to no longer apply. Though this is not to say one cannot acquire wealth and fame by becoming a stellar chef or craftsman, but society, by way of defining success through educational attainment, generally discourages these rather quirky paths. So while one may blame Mr. Chen's unhappiness for choosing a career that has little relevance to his major of communications, society may have more to blame. After all, Mr. Chen and many other Chinese youths may not choose their career paths or university majors out of passion or interest, but out of pressure and necessity.

APPENDIX

SAMPLE PUBLIC SERVICE EXAM QUESTIONS

1. Which of the following is incorrect:
   a. Blood sugar rises after consuming food.
   b. Fasting for more than 12 hours will result in Hypoglycemia (low blood sugar levels).
   c. Pumpkin can suppress glucose intake and lower blood sugar levels.
   d. Insulin is the only naturally occurring hormone that can lower blood sugar levels.

2. Which of the following gas can cause acid rain and functions as a preservative:
   a. Carbon Dioxide
   b. Nitrogen Dioxide
   c. Sulfur dioxide
   d. Dinitrogen

3. Which of the following explanation is correct:
   a. Pandora's Box—everything is unpredictable
   b. Achilles' Heel—weakness in spite of overall strength
   c. Thucydides Trap—hidden risks behind a peaceful facade

d. Sword of Damocles—war between a rising power and a ruling power is inevitable

4. Which of the following choices is incorrect:
    a. Food is an important and major source of vitamin intake.
    b. Vitamin E is an antioxidant. Vitamin K can help strengthen the immunity system.
    c. Vitamins are classified as either water soluble or fat soluble. Vitamin D belongs to the latter group.
    d. Fresh Tomato, kiwi, and pepper contain rich vitamin C.

5. Which of the following is correct:
    a. Arabic numerals were invented by the Romans and brought into Asia by Arabic trader.
    b. The first successful capitalist revolution occurred in the Netherlands.
    c. India has the largest arable land in Asia.
    d. The Renaissance began in England.

6. Which of the following factors is most important in affecting food spoilage:
    a. Food composition
    b. Food moisture
    c. Storage environment temperature
    d. Storage environment humidity

7. Which of the following choices is incorrect:
    a. Lead is a major component of pencil.
    b. Cigarettes contain lead.
    c. Lead does not decompose inside human body.
    d. Adding lead to petroleum can prevent explosion.

8. Which of the following choices is incorrect:
    a. Ronnie O'Sullivan is a professional snooker player.
    b. Tiger Wood is a professional golf player.
    c. Roger Federer is a professional tennis player.
    d. Rafael Nadal is a professional baseball player.
9. Which of the following choices is incorrect:
    a. Corazon Aquino was the first female president in Asia.
    b. Gloria Macapagal Arroyo is a former president of the Philippines.
    c. Park Geun-hye's father once served as the president of South Korea.
    d. Yingluck Shinawatra served as the Prime Minister of Malaysia.
10. Which of the following choices is incorrect:
    a. Montesquieu established the idea of three branches of government.
    b. Voltaire was the first philosopher to raise the concept of social contract.
    c. Plato advocated for a country ruled by a philosopher king.
    d. Jean Bodin is best known for his theory of sovereignty.
11. Adam, Brian, Cory, and David all want to take one month off between June and September, but the office needs three employees present at all time. David does not want to take June off. Adam does not want to take September off. Cory can take either June or August off, and Brian wants either July or August off. If requests by all four employees are met, which of the following can be deduced?
    a. Adam can only take June or July off.
    b. If Cory does not take June off, Brian must take July off.
    c. If Cory takes August off, Adam will take July off.
    d. If Brian takes July off, Cory will take June off.

12. Department A hired three new employees: Jack, John, and Jason. Employees Mary, Megan, and Margaret are told that their new colleagues have come one of three states: New York, Maryland, and Florida. The women guessed as follows:

Mary: Jack and Jason are from Florida. John comes from Maryland.

Megan: Jack comes from Florida. John comes from New York. Jason does not come from New York.

Margaret: Jack and Jason come from New York. John comes from Florida.

If Mary, Megan, and Margaret all guessed one piece of information regarding their new colleagues correctly, which of the follow is possible?

   a. Jack comes from New York. John comes from Maryland, and Jason comes from Florida.

   b. Jack comes from Florida. John and Jason come from New York.

   c. Jack comes from Maryland. John comes from Florida. Jason comes from New York.

   d. Jack comes from New York. John and Jason come from Maryland.

WORKS CITED

INTRODUCTION

Beijing Bureau of Statistics. 北京区域统计年鉴2019 (*Beijing Statistical Yearbook 2019*).Beijing: Beijing Bureau of Statistics, 2019.

Lan, Luan, Aimee Kim, Daniel Zipser, Minyi Su, Adrian Lo, Cherry Chen, and Cherie Zhang. *China Luxury Report 2019: How Young Chinese Consumers are Reshaping Global Luxury.* Shanghai: McKinsey Greater China's Apparel, Fashion and Luxury Group, 2019.

Ponciano, Jonathan. "The Countries with the Most Billionaires." Forbes, April 8, 2020.

Poverty Reduction and Economic Management Department. *From Poor Areas to Poor People: China's Evolving Poverty Reduction Agenda: An Assessment of Poverty and Inequality in China.* Beijing: The World Bank, 2009.

The World Bank Data. "GDP per Capita (Current US$) - China." Accessed August 5, 2020.

Xinhua News. "北京城镇单位年人均工资94258元(Annual Average Salary in Beijing Reaches 94,258 RMB)." May 31, 2019.

Xinhua News. "国务院总理李克强回答中外记者提问(Premier Li Keqiang Answers Questions from Chinese and Foreign Journalists)." May 28, 2020.

CHAPTER 1

D' Arpizio, Claudia, Federica Levato, Filippo Prete, Elisa Del Fabbro, and Joëlle de Montgolfier. *Luxury Goods Worldwide Market Study, Fall-Winter 2018*. Boston: Bain & Company, 2019.

Li, Hongbing, Prashant Loyalka, Scott Rozelle, Binzhen Wu, and Jieyu Xie. "Unequal Access to College in China: How Far Have Poor, Rural Students Been Left Behind?" *The China Quarterly,* no. 211 (March 2015): 185-207.

Ministry of Education of the People's Republic of China. "2019年全国教育事业发展统计公报(2019 Report on the Development of National Education Work)." Published May 20, 2020.

CHAPTER 2

Airui Guide. "2019年合肥市市直事业单位最终31816人参加考试(Hefei State-owned Institute Had 31,816 Applicants Taking Entrance Examination)." Published August 9, 2019.

Bjorklund, E. M. "The Danwei: Socio-Spatial Characteristics of Work Units in China's Urban Society." *Economic Geography* 62 no. 1 (January 1986): 19-29.

Bray, David. *Social Space and Governance in Urban China: the Danwei System from Origin to Reform*. Stanford: Stanford University Press, 2005.

Chai Weiyan, Xiao Zuopeng, Liu Tianbao, and Tana. 中国城市的单位透视(*China's Urban Danwei*). Nanjing: Southeast University Press, 2016.

Goffman, Erving. *Asylum: Essays on the Social Situations of Mental Patients and Other Inmates*. New Brunswick: Aldine Transaction, 2009.

He, Zhongda and Lü Bin. "中国单位制度社会功能的变迁(Evolution of the *Danwei* System's Societal Functions)." 城市问题 (*Urban Problems*) 26, no 11 (November 2007): 48-56.

Li, Hanlin and Li Lulu. 中国的单位组织: 资源、权力与交换(*China's Danwei System: Resource, Power, and Exchange*). Beijing: Life Bookstore Publishing, 2019.

Li, Hanlin. 中国单位社会: 议论、思考与研究(*Thoughts on Chinese Work-unit Society*). Shanghai: Shanghai People's Publishing House, 2004.

Li, Lulu. "论'单位'研究(Danwei Study)." *Sociological Studies* 17 no. 5 (May 2002): 23-32.

Liu, Zhenyun. 一地鸡毛(*Ground Covered with Chicken Feathers*). Wuhan: Changjiang Literature Publishing House, 1993.

———. 单位(*Danwei*). Wuhan: Changjiang Literature Publishing House, 1988.

Lü, Xiaobo and Elizabeth J. Perry. "Introduction." In *Danwei: The Changing Chinese Workplace in Historical and Comparative Perspective,* edited by Xiaobo Lü and Elizabeth J. Perry, 3-17. New York: M. E. Sharpe, 1997.

Sil, Rudra. "The Russian 'Village in the City' and Stalinist System of Enterprise Management: The Origins of Worker Alienation in Soviet State Socialism." In *Danwei: The Changing Chinese Workplace in Historical and Comparative Perspective*, edited by Xiaobo Lü and Elizabeth J. Perry, 114-141.New York: M. E. Sharpe, 1997.

Walder, Andrew G. *Communist Neo-Traditionalism: Work and Authority in Chinese Industry.* Berkeley: University of California Press, 1986.

Xinhua News. "中华人民共和国公务员法(Civil Servant Law of the People's Republic of China)," December 30, 2018.

CHAPTER 3

Anonymous User. Answer to "月薪一万在合肥能过什么样的生活? (What Kind of Lifestyle Can One Afford in Hefei with A Monthly Salary of 10,000 RMB?" Zhihu. Updated June 21, 2017.

China Power Team. "How Well-off is China's Middle Class." China Power. Updated October 29, 2020

Jinyuan Investment Group and Hurun Report. 2018 中国新中产圈层白皮书(China New Middle Class Report). Shanghai: Hurun Report, 2018.

Xinhua News. "哈尔滨3000大学生争考清洁工称没勇气拒绝(Over 3,000 College Graduates Compete for A Janitor Post, Claiming that They Do not Have the Courage to Reject)." November 2, 2012.

Zhaopin (智联招聘). 2020年冬季中国雇主需求与白领人才供给报告(*Report on Employers Demand and White-Collar Talents Supply in Winter of 2020*). Beijing: Zhaopin, 2020.

CHAPTER 4

Bian, Yanjie, Zhang Wenhong, and Cheng Cheng. "A Social Network Model of the Job-Search Process: Testing A Relational Effect Hypothesis." *Chinese Journal of Sociology*32, no. 3 (2012): 24-37.

Bian, Yanjie. "Guanxi Capital and Social Eating: Theoretical Models and Empirical Analyses," in *Social Capital: Theory and Research*, edited by Lin Nan, Ronald S Burt, and Karen S Cook, 276-297. New York: Aldine de Gruyter, 2001.

Earley, P. Christopher. *Face, Harmony, and Social Structure: An Analysis of Organizational Behavior Across Cultures*. Oxford: Oxford University Press, 1997.

Fei, Xiaotong. *From the Soil: The Foundations of Chinese Society*. Berkeley: University of California Press, 1992.

Granovetter, Mark S. *Getting a Job: A Study of Contacts and Careers* (Chicago: University of Chicago Press, 1974.

———. "The Strength of Weak Ties." *American Journal of Sociology* 78, no. 6 (May 1973): 1260-1380.

Kerley, Paul. "What is your 21st Century Social Class?" BBC, December 7, 2015.

Lin, Nan. *Social Capital: A Theory of Social Structure and Action.* Cambridge: Cambridge University Press, 2001.

The Beijing News. "河北大学撞人案疑犯涉交通肇事罪被刑拘(Suspect Involved in the Hebei University Homicide Detained)." October 19, 2010.

Yang, Mayfair Mei-hui. *Gifts, Favors, and Banquets: The Art of Social Relationships in China.* Ithaca: Cornell University Press, 1994.

Zhong, Lena Y. *Communities, Crime and Social Capital in Contemporary China.* London: Routledge, 2008.

CHAPTER 5

Research Group for The Language Situation in China. 中国语言生活状况报2006 (*The Language Situation in China 2006*). Beijing: Commercial Press, 2007.

Simpson, Peter. "The 'Leftover' Women: China Defines Official Age for Females Being Left on the Shelf as 27," *Daily Mail*, February 21, 2013.

The Paper. "我们去了相亲角6次，收集了这874份征婚启事(We Went to Matchmaking Corner Six Times and Collected 874 Marriage Posters)." August 17, 2018.

Zeng, Yuli. "Turn Off, Drop Out: Why Young Chinese Are Abandoning Ambition." Six Tone. Published July 27, 2017.

Zong, Zhiyuan, Li Yun, Wang Siyi, Zhang Yan, and Wang Ganli. 她，为什么' 剩下' ？——2016 中国城市"剩女"问题大数据研究报告(*Why Is She Leftover? 2016 Urban China "Leftover Women" Research Report*). Guangdong: Yangcheng Evening News, 2016.

CHAPTER 6

Chen, Yang. "央行调查报告：52%居民认为房价高(Central Bank Survey Report: 52% of Residents Think Housing Price Too High)." *The Beijing News*, December 25, 2015.

Numbeo. "Property Prices Index by Country 2019." Accessed January 16, 2021.

People's Daily. "房奴必须付出的代价：透支青春和父母的晚年(The Price Mortgage Slaves Must Pay: Overdrawing Their Youth and Their Parent's Post-Retirement Years)." December 3, 2012.

Xin'an Real Estate. "十二年蝶变！合肥房价究竟涨了多少？(Dramatic Change in 12 Years. How Much Did Housing Prices in Hefei Increase?)." Published December 17, 2020.

CHAPTER 7

Li, Hanlin and Li Lulu. 中国的单位组织：资源、权力与交换(*China's Danwei System: Resource, Power, and Exchange*). Beijing: Life Bookstore Publishing, 2019.

Li, Lulu. "论'单位'研究(Danwei Study)." *Sociological Studies* 17 no. 5 (May 2002): 23-32.

Ritzer, George. *The McDonaldization of Society*. 20th Anniversary ed. London: Sage Publications, 2013.

Shaw, Victor N. *Social Control in China: A Study of Chinese Work Units*. Westport: Praeger Publishers, 1996.

Zhang, Chun and Yanwei Chai. "Un-gated and Integrated Work Unit Communities in Post-Socialist Urban China: A Case Study from Beijing." *Habitant International* 43 (March 2014): 79-89.

CHAPTER 8

BBC. "Liang Jun: China's First Female Tractor Driver, and National Icon, Dies." January 15, 2020.

Ke, Meng. "毛泽东遗产争议：妇女能顶半边天(Controversies over Mao's Legacy: Women Hold up Half of the Sky)." BBC, December 24, 2013.

Lavely, William, Xiao Zhenyu, Li Bohua and Ronald Freedman. "The Rise in Female Education in China: National and Regional Patterns," *The China Quarterly* no. 121, 61-93.

Mackie, Gerry. "Ending Footbinding and Infibulation: A Convention Account." *American Sociological Review* 61, no. 6 (December 1996): 999-1017.

People's Daily. "中华人民共和国婚姻法(Marriage Law of the People's Republic of China)." April 16, 1950.

Quan, Hong. "The Representation and/or Repression of Chinese Women: From A Socialist Aesthetics to Commodity Fetish," *Neohelicon* 46 (2019): 717-737.

Zhou, Xiaoli. "中国女性的身体与革命性(The Body and Revolutionary Spirit of Chinese Women)." Intellectuals. Published March 30, 2018.

Zuo, Jiping. "20世纪50年代的妇女解放和男女义务平等：中国城市夫妻的经历与感受(Women's Liberation and Equality in Male-Female Responsibilities in the 1950s: Experience of Urban Couples in China)," *Chinese Journal of Sociology* 25, no. 1 (2005): 182-209.

CHAPTER 9

Hanser, Amy. *Service Encounter: Class, Gender, and the Market for Social Distinction in Urban China.* Stanford: Stanford University Press, 2008.

Human Rights Watch. *"Only Men Need Apply": Gender Discrimination in Job Advertisements in China.* New York: Human Rights Watch, 2018.

World Economic Forum. *The Global Gender Gap Report 2018.* Geneva: World Economic Forum, 2018.

Xiu, Lin and Morley Gunderson. "Gender Earnings Differences in China: Base Pay, Performance Pay, and Total Pay," *Contemporary Economic Policy* 31, no. 1 (2013): 235-254.

Yangpeng, Zheng. "Chinese Women Earn A Fifth Less Than Men and The Gap Is Widening Fast, Survey by Online Recruiter Boss Zhipin Finds." *South China Morning Post*, March 7, 2019.

CHAPTER 10

Human Rights Watch. *"Only Men Need Apply": Gender Discrimination in Job Advertisements in China.* New York: Human Rights Watch, 2018.

Leftover Women. Directed by Shosh Shlam and Hilla Medalia. Boston: PBS, 2019. Aired on PBS.

National Bureau of Statistics. "2018年全国时间利用调查公报 (Report on National Time Usage in 2018)." Published January 25, 2019.

National Health and Family Planning Commission. 2013中国卫生统计年鉴(*China Health Statistics Yearbook 2013*). Beijing: National Health and Family Planning Commission, 2013.

Vanham, Peter. "Women in China Contribute More to GDP than in the US. Viewing Them as 'Leftover' is Problematic." World Economic Forum. Published April 12, 2018.

CHAPTER 11

Hobcraft, John, Jane Menken, and Samuel Preston. "Age, Period, and Cohort Effects in Demography: A Review." In *Cohort Analysis in Social Research*, edited by William M. Mason and Stephen E. Fienberg, 89-135. New York: Springer, 1985.

Notestein Frank W., Irene B. Taeuber, Dudley Kirk, Ansley J. Coale, and Louise K. Kiser, *The Future Population of Europe and the Soviet Union: Population Projections, 1940-1970*. Geneva: League of Nations, 1944.

Southern Metropolis Daily. "养孩成本TOP10城市曝光：养个孩子消灭一个百万富翁(Top 10 Cities by Cost of Raising a Child: Raising a Child Can Destroy a Millionaire)."September 20, 2016.

Whittaker, D. Hugh, Tianbao Zhu, Timothy Sturgeon, Mon Han Tsai, and Toshie Okita. "Compressed Development." *Studies in Comparative International Development* 45 (2010): 439-467.

CHAPTER 12

Duara, Prasenjit. *Culture, Power, and the State: Rural North China, 1900–1942*. Stanford: Stanford University Press, 1998.

Geertz, Clifford. *Agricultural Involution: The Processes of Ecological Change in Indonesia*. Berkeley: University of California Press, 1969.

Huang, Phillip C. C. *The Peasant Economy and Social Change in North China*. Stanford: Stanford University Press, 1988.

Lianhe Zaobao. "小学生研究癌症相关基因或将被质疑造假(Primary School Students Who Won Awards for Research on Cancer-Related Genes Questioned for Forgery)." July 17, 2020.

National Business Daily. "小学生研究基因与癌症关系拿大奖，5天学会专业知识，水平堪比博士! 父母身份曝光... (Primary School Student Won Big Prize with Research on the Cancer and Gene. Mastered Expertise in Five Days Rivaling PhDs)." July 13, 2020.

NetEast News. "海淀家长和顺义妈妈的鸡娃史，一场父母的集体焦虑，如何破解困局(The History of Haidian Parents and Shunyi Moms, A Collective Anxiety Among Chinese Parents)." September 16, 2020.

NetEast News. "青少年科技创新大赛充斥着大量研究癌症、基因、细菌的中小学生(Youth Innovation Competition Filled with Primary and Middle School Students Researching Cancer, Genes, and Bacteria)." July 21, 2020.

People's Daily. "2020年十大流行语揭晓(Ten Most Popular Phrases in 2020)." December 5, 2020.

Sohu News. "上海10所最热门私立幼儿园! (Top 10 Private Kindergartens in Shanghai! Preparing)." August 17, 2018.

Tencent News. "出生就要排队! 上海10所热门幼儿园青浦独占其3，入园攻略曝光! (Waiting in Line Since the Day of Birth! Top 10 Private Kindergartens in Shanghai and the How to Guide)." March 10, 2020.

The Paper. "幼儿园已经开始内卷了(Involution Has Begun in Kindergartens)."October 14, 2020.

The Paper. "清华学生边骑车边用电脑? 当事人: 因害怕关闭机盖程序中断(Tsinghua Student Using Laptop While Riding Bike? Student Claims Afraid of Program Interruption)." September 30, 2020.

Xinhua News. "真的要把孩子变成'鸡娃'吗? (Should We Really Use 'Chicken Blood Therapy' on Children?)." December 16, 2019.

Xuandi, Wang. "Socially Dead Laborers of Versailles: China's 2020 in Memes," Sixth Tone. Published December 11, 2020.

Made in the USA
Columbia, SC
29 November 2021

50006899R00109